From GED to PhD

The Autobiography
of
Dr. Bon Blossman

Zakkem Publishing www.zakkempublishing.com

ISBN-13: 978-0-9850363-2-4

AUTHOR'S NOTE

Except for my family members, the names and some identifying details of the other people in this book have been changed. These are my accounts of the events in my life.

CONTENTS

Never give up. Conquer all.

ACKNOWLEDGMENTS

I express my enormous appreciation to my parents for being who they are – loving, generous, caring people. I would not change one thing about either of them or the way that they raised me. I appreciate everything in the world that they have done for me and their undying love and support. My parents are my inspiration to succeed. Another colossal thank you goes out to my brother Eric for always being there for me. He is the best brother I could have asked for, and I love him and his awesome family. I thank my husband Jason for being an essential part of my life. Jason is my unquestionable soul mate. We have had an incredible journey together thus far and may we have tons more adventures to come. I couldn't ask for more out of a partner in life. I thank my kids Whitney and Zakk for being my everything. My kids enrich my life every day and I've enjoyed every second that I've shared with both of them. Words cannot express how deeply I care for my children. Paola & Scot, Lora & Frank, and Sylvia & Jesse are my dearest friends. I appreciate how each one of them enhances my life and I appreciate each one of them for being who they are. I consider these people my extended family.

PREFACE

I am not Lucille Ball, Benjamin Franklin or Gandhi. I am not a survivor of slavery or the Holocaust. Why in a million light years would you want to hear my story? I guess you could say that I'm a statistical outlier that has beaten the odds. The fact that my high school GPA might have made it to a 1.8 before I dropped out and the reality that I was pregnant at seventeen and married at the courthouse in a black maternity dress might be of interest. However, these types of bad decision makers are unfortunately common in our society. What makes me stand out from my teenage cohort is that I have triumphed over self-afflicted hurdles in my life and overcame the consequences of my dreadful decisions to become what I am today. I am a mother of two beautiful children, have been married for eighteen years to my soul mate, and am a novelist with the title of *Dr.* before my name.

I wish to bundle my experiences and express them in one collective place in hopes to motivate others that find themselves in similar circumstances that I encountered in my past. I want to encourage our youth to become

1

whatever they desire in life. Just because somebody has done poorly for a year of high school or college – doesn't mean that their career path is wrecked, and they are destined to become a lifelong unemployed duck feeder.

I am writing this book for anybody who wants to learn more about me or better yet, learn from my mistakes, and my victories. If you are a teen, maybe I can get you on the right path. If you are an adult who veered away from your occupational trajectory, possibly I can inspire you to get back in the game. You shouldn't settle for anything that you feel mediocre about – always reach for the stars. Broken dreams lower your internal self-worth and keep you from taking risks that can have big payoffs. I want to aspire you to follow your dreams.

I'm not saying I'm perfect and have all the answers to the universe. I am not the most successful person nor have I reached my potential. I am far from that, for sure. My history of mistakes is definitely not a blueprint that you should follow for your future. However, you can use my experiences and missteps in life to arm yourself with knowledge about your own experiences.

If you want to be a doctor, lawyer, astronaut – it is within your reach and it is never too late. If you want to start a business, you have no excuse not to start today. Avoid growing elderly with regrets. No matter how old you may be, I aspire to help you to start focusing on your dreams. I desire to prompt you to live for yourself and take advantage of as many opportunities as you encounter. Opportunity can be hidden in a wicked disguise sometimes, so you'll need to sharpen up your skills to recognize it when it comes.

CHAPTER 1 - NEVER A QUITTER

I was born a first generation Texan. I grew up in an affluent neighborhood across from the golf course of Shady Oaks Country Club in Westover Hills, Texas. As of the year 2000, Westover Hills was ranked the wealthiest location in Texas per capita and the 12th highest in the United States. It is a quaint town of about 600 people completely surrounded by a larger metropolitan area known as the Dallas-Fort Worth (DFW) metroplex. I grew up as the baby of the family with loving parents, an older sister and brother, and a very large home with over an acre of a landscaped backyard.

My father was an established surgeon and I always had more than I needed. I realize that growing up wealthy might not make me relatable to most people, but believe me; I will show you just how relatable that I am throughout the course of my story.

I started taking dance lessons when I was four years old. My earliest memory was on stage during a recital. After we performed our dance, I was to make a train with the other dancers in my class by grabbing the girl's waist in front of me. We had rehearsed the exit from the stage and I was the caboose – a big mistake on the teacher's part. As the performance ended, I distinctly remember thoughts pouring through my head of not wanting to get off the stage. We made the train, I was the caboose, but I didn't exit the stage. Immediately as I neared the curtains, I dashed back to center stage and started doing my own dance. My fellow dancers looked on in horror as the crowd entered a hysteria, which made me dance even faster and goofier. I loved the attention until my dance teacher rushed over and escorted me off the stage. She wasn't happy to say the least. That's where the memory ends.

I mention this event because it sets the stage, no pun intended, for my aptitude in life. It foreshadows my struggles with authority, proves that being the center of attention is an innate characteristic, and is not always a negative thing.

Throughout my early education, I was a good student. I had straight A's but with slight problems in conduct. I couldn't stop talking during class. It didn't matter where the teacher put me in the classroom; I would make new friends and fire up new conversations. It wasn't necessarily a matter of disrespect for the teacher; it was an incurable urge to socialize, leading to my ultimate inclination for party hosting. I think they might refer to the behavior as *Attention Deficit Disorder* today, but back then, it was labeled as *misconduct*.

My parents looked the other way on slight divergences in behavior as long as my grades were excellent. My advice when you have kids – punish them for less than perfect marks in behavior. Not that I'm trying to be a buzz kill to future generations, but life is about learning from experiences, and if I would have been punished for misbehaving at an earlier age, I *might* not have found myself in as much trouble later. However, to be honest, this is a big *might* because I am more than strong headed.

During my childhood years, I engaged in acting lessons, tennis lessons, golf lessons, karate classes, roller-skating speed team, gymnastics lessons, Girl Scouts, as well as dance classes. I was a member of Shady Oaks Country Club, competed with the Shady Oak's swim team, and attended the club's summer day camp each summer. I was also a runway model for Neiman Marcus at various fashion shows at our country club. I was a very busy child, well behaved, and I strongly believe that those two things are correlated.

Today, I am a horrible golfer and as a child, I was intermediate at best. I remember the infamous Ben Hogan, who was a charter member of our country club and is a legendary gold professional. I was at the golf pro shop one day and noticed a sign up sheet for private golf lessons by Ben Hogan for the kids of the club. Not knowing he was a legendary golf superstar, I jotted my name down on the list and later told my mother that I had a 1-hour lesson scheduled for the following weekend with a golf pro. I remember my mother, who had found out who the golf pro was, instructed me to refer to him as Mr. Hogan as I took off to the golf course for my private lesson. The lesson was great, Mr. Hogan was a super guy, and all I can remember from that hour is Mr. Hogan instructing me how to hold my club. He did teach me a lot more in that private lesson, but my brain is older and cannot remember the fine details. To this day, I don't take well to people instructing me on how to hold a club, as I learned from the best. Even if I've forgotten what he showed me, and I'm doing it wrong, I don't want anybody tainting what this icon taught me that day. There is another funny twist to this Ben Hogan story later when I talk about my husband Jason. Stay tuned for more of the Hogan saga.

Nevertheless, I was fortunate to have the lifestyle that afforded me tremendous opportunities. As a child, my mother taught me not to quit, even when my heart wasn't into what I was doing. The one thing she reluctantly allowed me to quit still bothers me today.

I took acting lessons and acted in plays at Casa Manana in Fort Worth, Texas for many years as a child. As part of the class, I was eventually assigned to perform a duet for an upcoming competition with a boy. Simultaneously, my two girl friends in the class were assigned to perform a duet together. I didn't think that was fair and pouted as I read my assigned script under protest. After reading the script, I asked my teacher what a coquette was because that was the description of my character. He responded that it was a flirtatious girl and I winced, as I wasn't happy with his answer. I read further and in the script, I was to kiss this boy after flirting with him for a few minutes on a park bench. I was mortified, as I was only eleven years old and very shy around boys. I went home and told my mother I wasn't doing the duet and she responded that if I didn't do it, it wasn't meant to be, and that I would have to resign from acting altogether. Begrudgingly, I agreed to quit. She made me quit in person, which at that time, was the hardest thing I ever had to do. I showed up to Casa Manana the day of our duet rehearsal and walked past a birthday cake on the table for my duet partner. I felt horrible, but I told him and the teacher that I was quitting the class that day. From that day forth, I was never in another play or acting class, and I still feel miserable that I quit and gave up on my acting career.

That miserable feeling from quitting stayed with me and I never wanted to start something that I didn't intend on finishing from that day forward. Alternatively, I can see how someone could fall into a pattern of quitting after 'breaking the quitter ice' like that and the behavior could become the norm. I've seen that in many teens and young adults with entry-level jobs - how it becomes acceptable to quit when things get rough instead of sticking to it and working their way up the career ladder.

My opinion is that you need to finish what you start as a child or you'll be more likely to quit things as an adult. However, it's never too late to turn it around and change your habit. If you feel that you are likely to quit projects, make a change. Start with something small like a two-week course at the local recreation center in another language, or maybe a cooking class at a health food store, and force yourself to complete it. Then, your record starts over and you have a fresh sense of accomplishment. You won't want to break that record.

Points to Ponder: If you decide to start something, you should always finish what you started. Even if you plan never to do it again, you'll have a sense of accomplishment that will ignite a routine of task completion.

CHAPTER 2 - FASHION FRIENDSHIPS

At this time, I refuse to obsess over designer labels on my clothing. I appreciate a nicely made article of clothing and I own my share of designer threads. However, I decline to be concerned with what other people are wearing. It's great if you want a $2000.00 Christian Dior pair of shoes – God knows I want many of them. If you can afford them and they make you feel good – then get 'em. However, if owning the shoes causes you to become judgmental of others who do not have the same caliber of shoes, you need to rethink your outlook on life and realize what is important.

I love fashion. Clothes make me feel good and I love dressing up and following trends. Don't get me wrong – I'm just like the next girl when it comes to getting the new styles each season. Runway models are meant to be judged on fashion, but fellow guests at a party should be off limits. My opinion is other than the runways; keep your eyes in the mirror if you are trying to critique fashion.

Here's a hypothetical example of a fashion rule. You have reservations for a five star restaurant. There's a dress code and you're expected to wear a cocktail dress. It shouldn't matter if you purchased the cocktail dress at a cheap teenage store or at Neiman Marcus – if you are wearing what is required and you feel good about it, that's fantastic. Nobody has the right to judge your clothing. On the other hand, if you walk into the restaurant for the same reservation wearing a heavy metal t-shirt and short camouflage shorts with your booty hanging out, be prepared to be judged and asked to leave to change your attire. There *are* a few fashion rules in our society in which you must abide.

My story of being a fashion snob is brief, yet shocking. In elementary school, everything I owned had a designer label. Ralph Lauren, Gloria Vanderbilt, Calvin Klein, Guess and Izod were the top designers for kid's clothes at the time. If you have to wonder who some of those designers are, you are just too young, trust me. In my group, you were only supposed to wear Bass penny loafers or Topsider deck shoes. I only shopped at Neiman Marcus or another designer boutique called Henry's. If it didn't have a designer label, it wasn't getting on my body or I would have thrown a massive fit resembling a seizure.

Let's get to a bleak part of my life where a horrible personality began to form inside of me. I was a product of my environment, not at home, but at my school. My good friends wore designer clothes. It was nearly like a cult of little girls following *The Official Preppy Handbook* as a manual of life. If you strayed away from our group's fashion rules, you were shunned. This situation, looking from the outside, was entirely sad. I cannot believe that I was a part of this way of life. I am ashamed of my past brain and how it was able to think in this judgmental, cliquish manner. I am embarrassed to have been part of a group resembling the movie *Mean Girls*.

There are two horrible events I must get off my chest before I can move on to motivate you to succeed. I hope that you can learn from my mistakes and see the world differently if you have any of these fashion snob tendencies. We all make mistakes in life and as children; we may not realize the ramifications of our actions. I don't blame anybody else for my behavior. I was 100% responsible for my actions.

I had a very dear friend in elementary school. We did absolutely everything together, including shopping for school clothes. Her parents were not as wealthy as mine were, but as a kid, I didn't realize the difference. I remember shopping with her and recall her mother saying they were not able to afford the same clothing as I had purchased for school. We ended up with the same wardrobe, which was most likely a financial strain on her parents. We wanted to dress alike, and our larger group had fashion rules of which we had to follow.

The following year, another wardrobe-shopping event took place. I didn't realize that at some point, her mother had purchased a replica of the Izod shirt. It was a J.C. Penney Fox shirt. Instead of the alligator, it had a fox, but it appeared to be a copy of the Izod line. Since we dressed alike on most days, my friend wore the same color Fox shirt to match to my Izod shirt. I couldn't understand what would compel her to wear this fashion travesty to school. At least my immature, bratty mind thought it was a fashion travesty. My memory is slightly fuzzy on whether I confronted her about the Fox shirt or if I simply drifted away as a friend swiftly without explanation. Either way, it was the mark of the end of our friendship on my end. I cannot apologize enough for my horrid behavior.

I really want to go back in time and kick my own ass for being so foolish and judgmental. It is more than appalling to treat others differently because of their clothing. It is atrocious behavior for kids and even worse for adults that still live in that fashion snob world.

Let's move on to my eleventh birthday. My parents were showering me with gifts as usual. My father had done some of my birthday shopping and in one of the packages was a J.C. Penny Fox shirt. Brutal irony slapped me in the face as I opened the box. I immediately rushed to my room, and a tantrum ensued for a long period. Again, if there are ever time machines invented, I will definitely go back and kick my own ass - not once, but multiple times. Not that I believe in violence, but a future self beating up a past self is considered legal. Well, it should be legal, nonetheless. I will worry about lobbying for the laws if time machines are ever invented.

My parents, I am sure, felt awful for making me upset on my birthday. I think they should have punished me for being a horrible soul and not being appreciative for getting a present! It was a clean case of karma biting me in the face for being more than ugly to a friend about the JC Penny Fox shirt. My dad thought the shirt was what we wore; he didn't know the difference between the two designers. Why would he care? He had people's lives to save as a surgeon. That's what really mattered, anyway. Once again, I hereby apologize to my parents for being an awful-hearted spoiled child. I should have sucked it up and wore the shirt to show appreciation for the present and to support my friend that I had wronged. However, I didn't do either of those things. Instead, my father and I took an immediate trip to Neiman Marcus to get new shirts. Ugh, I despise my past self! Really! This saint of a man who dedicated time and money to orphans had to rush to Neiman Marcus with his daughter to make right on a birthday present. Where was *his* karma that day?

11

Therefore, I cringe every time I see somebody flaunting their clothes or judging others for what they are wearing. It's one thing to be passionate about fashion, but another to be concerned with what anybody else's fashion choices are and to treat them differently for what they wear. Say what you will behind their back, it's only making your soul turn black. However, if you feel compelled to approach another person about what they have on their body, you are contaminated with evil and need to seek an exorcist.

There are fashion events where you are expected to be judged, however. It's a tradition with many people to buy the most festive Easter dress and at Sunday morning service, you flaunt the dresses around and this is all in fun. That is acceptable and you expect to be judged. My point that I'm driving home is when you purchase high fashion items at big-ticket prices, it doesn't make your internal self worth go up a bit – you're still the same person on the inside as you were before.

In life, what is important is health and love coupled with getting the most out of life, helping others, and having fun. It shouldn't matter if you wear a toga, a costume from party city, Old Navy garb or Neiman Marcus rags – clothing is clothing and that's that. Be glad you don't have to run around naked and barefoot.

Points to Ponder: Never judge others for what they have. You should only be concerned with what is going on with you, your family, your backyard and your closet. Strive to help others in life instead of breaking them down.

CHAPTER 3 - BAD INFLUENCE

At the close of my fifth grade year, I sat in the cafeteria with my fellow female students. It felt strange that we were separated from the boys. Our teachers acted strangely, ultra-secretive, telling us that what we were about to watch was very important. I was so curious - what was so important and why couldn't the boys be there?

The projector fired up and the film blasted on the big screen. The narrator described a girl's body and the anatomical and physiological changes that occur as she develops. A roar of giggles ensued and nobody in the cafeteria took it seriously. It was a medically based film that didn't relate to us, and we all felt awkward. I wanted nothing more but for it to stop.

I didn't pay attention to the discussion of menstruation and the ovarian cycles as my best friends were doing their best to distract us all from the awkwardness. I had heard about such a thing from a friend's hippie mother already and it freaked me out tremendously. So be it. I told my mother about the strange film experience and she handed me a medical textbook. It was a fitting response since she was a registered nurse and my father was a surgeon. Medical textbooks were everywhere in my house.

The book was opened to the chapter about menstruation. I was confused; I needed to know more about this? At this point, I felt gross and scared about what was going to happen to me in the future. However, I turned a few pages and it went on about the human reproductive system. I felt ashamed for looking at it, shut the book, never to look at it again.

I didn't grow up in an open home where we mentioned anything about reproduction or sex in any manner. In my home, it wasn't expected that kids would know about it, talk about it and certainly would never try it. With the power of hindsight, I think it is imperative in today's society to be open with your kids when the time is right. Explain things in a way they can understand without making them feel uncomfortable. Maybe if you don't feel comfortable doing it, hire a local teen to be a mentor and filter information through to them. In any case, the information about disease and pregnancy needs to get to our kids, at an appropriate age, through somebody they trust.

That's my background on sex education. Very limited and inadequate. I made my own decisions later, but had I been armed with a better understanding, I believe I could have avoided a pregnancy at the young age of seventeen. My mother grew up naive and I don't blame her in the least. She was an awesome mom. She just didn't think in a billion light years that her kids, including me, would think to do such a thing that early in life.

Sex wasn't my problem at this time in my life as I was too scared of it. Probably because I hadn't met the wrong boy that made a strong enough push for it. My problems leading to a self-destructive journey began with experimentation with harmful substances. There is the critical importance of kids having a focus in life and staying busy.

By seventh grade, my extra-curricular activities dwindled down to one dance class per week. Swim team season had ended and there was nothing to keep my idle mind busy. Therefore, my friends and I started getting into trouble. Back then, you could purchase cigarettes out of a vending machine. Of course, the machines were everywhere. What brilliant tobacco marketing executive thought of that, by the way?

One day, my friends and I bought cigarettes out of boredom. We thought we were cool and grown up by smoking these cigarettes. My mother and aunt both smoked cigarettes at the time, so I felt it was safe for me to smoke. I knew it was wrong, but I didn't care. I planned to blame my mom for setting the bad example and pry upon her guilt later if I were caught. How could she punish me when I could blame her as the reason why I chose to smoke cigarettes in the first place? Nonetheless, she didn't catch me until I was sixteen years old. By then, I was addicted. Again, I do not put any blame upon my mother for the reason why I smoked cigarettes. I was rebellious and I'm certain I would have done it anyway. The cigarette machine that we purchased cigarettes from was in the lobby of our favorite pizza place and it was only a matter of time before we got to it whether my mom smoked or not. If anything, I blame the tobacco executives for putting cigarettes within my reach as a minor. I'm glad they finally changed the laws where they can place these cigarette machines.

Unfortunately, cigarettes aren't where my harmful habits ended. My parents, who didn't drink alcohol on *any* occasion, had a fully stocked bar for parties that they hosted maybe once or twice a year. I didn't learn to drink alcohol by example here - so psychologists should have fun analyzing that one. My friends and I siphoned alcohol from their collection nearly every weekend, replacing it with water or tea. Who would complain to their boss for having weak drinks at his Christmas party? Nobody! It wasn't until my housekeeper at the time started showing up to work drunk that my mom started marking liquor bottles. After that, we had to switch strategies to flirting with older boys to con them into buying alcohol for us. That wasn't difficult as the drinking age at the time was only nineteen.

One by one, our local hangouts would banish my friends and me from their property. We were drunken adolescents, occasionally throwing up our wine coolers in their bathroom stalls. I don't blame them for kicking us out. I only blame them for not calling the police on us and making us accountable for our behavior. I have nobody to blame for my behavior, as I was the ringleader. I am a natural born leader and that can sometimes be a good or a bad thing depending upon the situation.

By the time I reached ninth grade, I was a party girl. The weekend would come and all we were concerned with was who was getting the booze, having cigarettes, and the location of the best party. We also tried marijuana a couple of times. I was lucky that I didn't like it, or I might have continued to use the stuff. I started the ninth grade year with all honors courses, as I had always previously been in the accelerated program. I had worked so hard in my previous years to maintain an excellent grade average in honors courses.

My grades started to plummet. I didn't want to study and all I wanted to do was talk on the phone. I didn't want to listen to my teachers anymore. They became boring to me and prevented me from socializing. I did whatever I could to be the class clown to make the time pass as quickly as possible, even drinking alcohol on occasion during class. Alas, the reason why I didn't completely fail my first semester of high school is that I have a photographic memory and when the teacher wrote things on the board, my neurons would capture enough information to pass the test. The sad thing is, failure was *necessary* for me at this point. It would have sent a large, neon flag to my parents that something was wrong. Instead, with C's and D's on my report card, I claimed the honors courses in high school were simply too difficult. I was a master manipulator.

The guidance counselor moved me out of the honors courses and I continued on my path of settling for average to poor grades. Even with this poor academic status, I was nominated and voted by my peers as the freshman Howdy Queen. I was popular and that is all that mattered to me at the time. However, if you ask the girls that merged with us into our high school campus from the other middle schools, I'm sure they'll come up with all kinds of reasons *why* I was elected Howdy Queen. I think that one of them had said that 'people felt sorry for me and that's why I won the vote.' Really? Sorry for me? I was voted as Howdy Queen in a school of 1800 people because people felt *sorry* for me? *(Lingering, arduous sigh inserted here.)* You may wonder why I bring up this issue. This was a life lesson in disguise. When you achieve things and enter the limelight, there are always people who are jealous of your success. If you plan on achieving great things in life – here is my stern warning: where there is success, there are haters. They go hand in hand and there's nothing you can do about it besides ignore it or embrace it. As far as the Howdy Queen title, there should have been a grade restriction on earning the title, by the way. Again, I'm begging for some retro punishment of my former self.

At a family member's wedding, my mother allowed me to have some champagne. She had no idea at this point that my friends and I were routinely drinking on the weekends. I continued to drink the entire wedding reception with a couple of my friends. As we graduated to playing a drinking game called 'quarters,' my older brother Eric sauntered over to give me a warning to stop making a scene. I remember walking over to my parent's friends from the country club and saying in a slurred voice that my parents allowed me to have champagne and that I was having a blast. I hereby give my parents a formal apology. It was more than wrong to behave that way, even if I was drunk, and I sucked really badly as a daughter for putting you through that. Nonetheless, I kept on drinking and eventually, my mother had to chase my drunken teenage self all over the ballroom as I picked up half full glasses of champagne from the tables and gulped them down. The day ended with me eating a turkey leg on my kitchen floor while my grandmother tried to feed me crackers. My mother wanted me to get sick to teach me a lesson about drinking. I never got sick that day and I felt wonderful the following day. Lesson learned, don't give your kids alcohol in hopes it will make them sick and they'll learn a lesson and not want to drink. Chances are, if your kids ask you for alcohol, it might be because they already drink it on occasion.

At this point in my life, I was raised in a structured home as a member of an affluent family. I had absolutely no reason to rebel or act in this manner and I certainly knew better. I respected my parents, but why did I behave this way? To be honest, I don't have the answer. I might have a gene that caused me to rebel and behave badly and if so, I definitely passed on the gene to my daughter.

There I was, on top of the world. I was loving life but not loving my future self to say the least. I had no academic motivation. Why not? Both of my parents were college-degreed. It's not as if they expected any less of me or that I didn't have a role model to follow.

I masked the fact that I was doing poorly in school by playing dumb. I was smart enough to know that if my parents believed that I was not intelligent, they wouldn't expect much out of me and would feel sorry for me that I was struggling academically. It worked for the most part, I claimed stupidity, and they released the noose a bit.

I did respect my parents. I wanted my parents to see me doing well and to be proud of me, but why did I choose such a self-destructive path? It might have been that the frontal cortex of my brain wasn't fully developed and I didn't have the power of consequence-driven thoughts yet. As a PhD student, I took a neurophysiology course focusing on the developing nervous system. My professor told me to be cautious getting mad at teens or young adults for making poor decisions because the frontal cortex of the brain is responsible for higher-ordered thought and consequence-driven perception, and it develops last. This part of the brain sometimes doesn't fully develop until you are in your twenties. Why does this part of your brain have to develop last, and why does it take so long to develop? Who knows the answer to that, but if you can figure out a way to have it develop quicker, you'll be rich.

Points to Ponder: Children should be armed with the proper information about their health, academics, friendships, before it is too late. Parent and child relationships need to be very open and honest with sex, drugs, and alcohol. Most of all, kids should stay very busy. A kid with idle time will find trouble eventually.

CHAPTER 4 - OFF TO THE ARMPIT

My mother was always the one to locate and bust up a party. She was the strict one and my father, the busy surgeon, was a loveable pushover. My mother didn't really get support from him as far as discipline goes because he worked a lot and was always on call. During his free time, he certainly didn't want to fill it with negative discipline toward his kids. It was awesome to have a dad like that, but I'm not so sure it lent itself to creating well-behaved kids. I'm certain that my bratty attitude stemmed from being a daddy's girl that was only disciplined by her mother. My mom's discipline was simply raising her voice and that wasn't very intimidating. Don't get me wrong, I was blessed to have my parents and I wouldn't trade them for the world with any other. There's no textbook manner of parenting that works in every situation and my parents did the best that they knew how. They were loving, supportive and cared a little too much about our feelings. It's always easy to look back on things and analyze where things might have gone wrong.

My father had always been a private practicing surgeon in Fort Worth Texas at his own clinic that included patient rooms, a pharmacy, a blood lab, x-ray rooms, EKG rooms, and traction machines. I spent every summer working as an assistant to everybody at the clinic and this is where I gained valuable medical experience. My father was also a dedicated Shriner (Shriner's Children's Hospital) and donated time to help the orphans living within the Masonic Home. I remember orphans visiting with us various weekends. We enjoyed having them and I hope they enjoyed staying with us. This is where I gained my love for humanity and appreciation for children – even though I was also a child at the time. My father had previously served in the U.S. Marine Core and continued with the National Guard. Years went by, his rank increased to colonel, and that's when my parents decided to move to Europe for a few years. A military life was looking promising and my father, having lost two brothers in the armed forces in Germany during World War II, was looking to serve our country as active duty as well. He put in a request to become active duty and relocate to Germany.

My parents asked me if I wanted to attend my senior year of high school in Europe. I was only fifteen and without a consequence-driven thought, I responded with a yes. Looking back, why did my parents ask my opinion? They were the adults and should have just made me do whatever they decided. It's easy for me to say that, however. I'm certain I was more than a hand full for them to deal with on a daily basis.

I agreed to live in Europe, knowing it was a few years away. To my despair, my parents didn't realize that my father would be asked to do a two-year stint at a military base in what I refer to be the armpit of America. No offense to the people of Wichita Falls, Texas, but compared to the metroplex and how I ended up being bullied in high school, I can't help but defend the title I created for the town. I still have friends that I cherish that live in the armpit, but living in the armpit is absolutely no reflection on a person. There just isn't that much to do as far as entertainment is concerned. In DFW, we have every restaurant imaginable, amusement parks, concert venues, nice museums, and the best shopping per capita. I was enrolled at one of the top dance studios in Fort Worth and at the time, Wichita Falls didn't have a dance studio with the same exposure. I'm not even sure if there was a country club in the armpit, but if so, it definitely wouldn't have held a candle to Shady Oaks. There aren't as many career opportunities in that town as compared with DFW. That's my main issues with the town. Again, many highly successful people are more than happy living there and I don't blame them, as it is a very community based, laid-back way of living. It just isn't for me.

Not wanting me to have to move immediately, my mom made an agreement to live away from my father during the week and drive to Wichita Falls to see him on the weekends. Why would she do this? Why would I allow my parents do this? It was very selfish behavior. I understand and appreciate that they didn't want to take me out of school with friends I had known most of my life. However, parents are the adults who make the decisions and if their decision was to move to Wichita Falls, I should have gone without a question and with a smile on my face and with a positive attitude. I am often ashamed of my past behavior, but it is what it is and so I tell the story.

In the middle of the spring semester, my mother told me that she didn't want to live apart from my father any longer and that I would need to move to Wichita Falls until we moved to Europe. This was more than devastating. I was to move out of the only house I ever knew and live in a city that I had never heard of with people that didn't know me. I was fifteen and struggling in school - a cigarette smoker who drank alcohol on the weekends. Some might say that moving could have been the best thing for a kid in my situation, but you will see, it was probably the worst.

My mother tried to cheer me up by saying that she would find a house with a pool. I nearly drowned when I was two and my father had to jump into the swimming pool, fully clothed, to retrieve me from the bottom of the deep end. She was afraid of water and even though we had an enormous back yard in the home that I grew up in and I was on a swim team, we never had a pool. She made an exception to her fear to allow me to have one of my own at the house in the armpit. I would not have to walk across the golf course to get to the country club pool. The pool would be in my back yard and that was great news. Nevertheless, another major problem for me was that there was no more country club.

There was a child-to-parent contract that I created. This was definitely another childhood issue of which I am ashamed. I wrote a contract for my parents to sign before I would agree to move to the armpit. In the contract was a monetary allowance for clothes and for the long distance phone bill to speak to my friends from DFW, my mother would have to drive me to Ft. Worth (2-hour drive) for private dance lessons on Saturday and allow me to spend the night on Saturday with my friends. Oh, and the last one is the kicker - my parents agreed to allow me to have a hardship license and own a car before I was sixteen.

Please don't put the book down because you hate me now. I know…it was ridiculous. There are many things that I did that I am ashamed of in my past. If you are a teen reader – please listen to how regretful I am for treating my parents this way. If you are a parent reader – don't put up with this nonsense from your kids.

I have no idea why they spoiled me this much over having to move cities. I suppose now that I know the outcome. It was a small price that they paid for the ultimate torture that ensued upon me. However, on the surface, I feel horrible for doing anything less than complying with their move with less than a smile on my face. I love my parents and think they are the most awesome people on the planet and I cannot say this enough. It's always easier with hindsight to see what the right thing we should have done would have been and our adult brains are far more rational.

We arrived at our new temporary house and it was about half the size of the one I grew up in, and it had a weird smell. Like *other people* smell. It was unfamiliar, like going into somebody else's house. I hated it. My fabulous gigantic maze of a house was no more. Now, I was in a home with a pool, but the home wasn't mine. What had defined me my entire life was non-existent.

We unpacked the boxes and as our things hit the rooms, it started to feel slightly better. However, it never felt the same. My room was depressing. The room that I had grown up in had a bright cheery yellow décor. My room in the armpit house was far different, yet it was fitting for the mood at hand. The color scheme was dark blue.

As a teen with both of my siblings out of the house, I had become an only child. At that point, I had minimal interaction with my siblings, nonetheless, as they were five and six years older than I was. My brother was my lovable antagonist who later became a best friend when we got older. My sister and I had very little interactions and she was out of the house by the time I was twelve. I guess you can attribute the minimal contact to growing up in a massive house, going to different schools, having zero personality traits and interests in common, and having different sets of friends.

My mother had previously kept the family on a rigorous schedule where she cooked three meals a day, ensured our baths and teeth were brushed on schedule, and bedtime was to the minute. By this time, the schedules wilted away and the structure in the home faded as I grew older and essentially, I became an only child. My mother still had no idea of my weekend partying and thought everything was fine with me and that I was doing what I was supposed to be doing. Little did she know the turmoil of rebellion that was brewing in my head.

The next item on our family task list was to find a new high school.

Points to Ponder: If possible, parents should avoid moving adolescent kids during the critical years of school (7th through the 11th grade). It is an emotionally sensitive period of life and can be disastrous to a kid's trajectory. However, when jobs or other circumstances cannot be avoided, kids should understand and respect their parents' situation.

CHAPTER 5 - HOWDY QUEEN TO MOST HATED

My dad met a friend and fellow colonel on the military base in the armpit. He had a daughter who attended a private Catholic school. Up until this point, I had been raised a very strict Catholic – attending CCD class and mass every Sunday. As I said before, as I grew older, the structure in our home faded and by this time, I didn't attend CCD classes anymore. I was introduced to this colonel's daughter and she seemed nice. However, she was wearing a mind-numbing uniform. At this time in my life, fashion was still very important to me. I knew that the uniform the chick was wearing definitely did not come from Neiman Marcus.

This *crime to fashion* garb was not going to cut it for me. In addition, this girl seemed *too* nice. She definitely didn't look like she smoked cigarettes, scouted out the best parties, and certainly didn't appear to have a taste for alcohol. She looked to be a bore and if this was what my life was turning into, I was not going to be all right. The princess tantrums ensued. I demanded to go to public school. I figured with my teenage brain that the coolest people would be there. My parents should have stood their ground and made me put on the uniform, be friends with this girl, and attend the private school. However, that's easy for me to say that now. Why was I so stubborn and why couldn't I see that this was a great opportunity to turn my life around? Had I gone this route, I can only assume that I'd have traveled a much easier road to get where I am today. I know I have the IQ and ambition; I just took the wrong path and continued to make it a journey into the wilderness of mistakes and bad-decisions.

On the other side, maybe this uniformed private schoolgirl was a promiscuous meth addict and I *did* take the right path by going to public school? Maybe there were secret drug rings at this private school and I would have been a pawn as the new girl. Well, probably not. A girl can dream and make up impossible scenarios to feel better about bad decisions, right?

My mother and I drove up to my future public high school and I caught a glimpse of a license plate on a Chevy Camero that said *BFDEAL*. I smiled. I knew instantly that this was the school for me. I knew what it stood for, but my naïve mom had no clue. I immediately exclaimed that I felt better about Wichita Falls and that I was happy to attend this school. My mom was glad that there was a smile on my face the first time since we had moved. She complied and enrolled me into the public school, which I later referred to as *Nightmare High*. My mother and I had a deal for the first week of school and she picked me up for lunch every day. I didn't have friends at school, but we both knew that I always had made friends easily. I agreed that if I met a friend and was comfortable, I could stay at school and eat in the cafeteria.

I walked into my first classroom of my new high school. The architecture was different from my previous school.

The desks were different. The faces were different. My heart thumped in my chest fiercely. Thirty pairs of eyes were glued to me, judging me. Nobody cracked a smile to make me feel at ease.

I was wearing matching Ralph Lauren polo attire from head to toe – including a ribbon in my hair with the polo emblem on it. Polo shirt, polo pants, polo socks and Bass penny loafers. I cautiously looked around at the others and noticed heavy metal t-shirts and not a designer piece of clothing in the room. I was out of place. I could tell immediately that I did not fit in. I thought to myself that maybe it was just the geometry class. I reasoned that maybe there were people like me in the school, but I just hadn't met them yet. As luck would have it, they were nowhere to be found. In fact, the comments that buzzed around the hallways were a confirmation of that fact that I didn't fit into this school. I was being ridiculed for my matching designer attire. I reiterate, judging someone for his or her clothing is highly inappropriate. This was a budding reason why I believe so strongly in karma. I had previously judged others for fashion and here I was, being judged. I deserved what I got at this moment in my life.

The rest of the morning was the same, but I started to get a few gazes from the boys in the hallways and in my classes. The girls continued to glare and grimace. This did not go well for me. In the hallway, I continued to search for other preppy girls. I held fast to the thought that there had to be a similar group of girls here at Nightmare High. I finally found a small group of what appeared to be preppy girls huddled by a locker in the hallway. I walked up to them, and they turned their backs to me. They whispered, turning around to smile at me with sarcasm. I realized immediately that they were not going to accept me into their clique. I hated high school. I really did. I still do today, actually. Some things in life, you'll never get over. I hope that one day; I can heal completely from it all. I also hope to dedicate a portion of my time to stop bullying (stay tuned) in schools. I know what it feels like not to be accepted. It is an awful, terrifying feeling to feel alone and embarrassed among your peers.

The lunch bell rang and I jetted outside to my mother's car. I jumped in, and clicked on the seatbelt with a full pout in motion. I explained to her how horrible everybody had been to me all day. She tried to smooth things over and say that it was the *first day jitters* and things would be fine. I moped around during my lunch hour before going back to what I eventually referred to as the *hell period*. This was my physical education class. I didn't like to exercise other than my dance classes and I hated sports. My prior physical education courses in school had always included my very best friends to make the exercising and silly games tolerable. Laughter made anything bearable. I knew right away that there would be no laughter for me in *this* course.

The first day of this class, I filed into the girl's locker room with the rest of the class and took a seat on the bench next to a row of lockers. Immediately, a very irate senior girl named Betty demanded that I take a seat in a chair in the middle of the room. Out of fear, I did what she asked me to do and I sat in the chair, perplexed. She proceeded to circle me like a shark, spouting statements such as *she isn't that pretty, look at her* and *she thinks she is so perfect but she is ugly*. The other girls either laughed or recoiled in fear. I'm assuming the laughing girls were her minions and the others were prior victims.

She was very incensed, angry with me for existing, and I had never seen her before that moment in the locker room. She threatened that she would take a picture of me with her

Polaroid camera as soon as I undressed, make copies of it, and post it all over the school.

I was required to wear a nasty uniform for the gym class. There was no way I was going to wear the atrocious articles of clothing that were assigned to me. There was no way I was going to undress in front of Betty the bully so she could humiliate me to the school by posting pictures of me in my underwear. Therefore, I refused to change clothes and sat on the bench. I got away with this for a few days until finally; someone told the teacher that I had been staying behind in the locker room during the class period. It was probably Betty that told on me. She was almost certainly looking for me in the gym to torture each day and I wasn't there. I was hiding in the locker room the entire class period until everybody left when class was over. During these three days, nothing had changed in the school experience for me. In fact, I became more frightened to walk in the halls.

On the fourth day, the P.E. teacher stormed into the locker room during the class period and found me hiding. She demanded to know why I wasn't changing into the gym uniform and participating in class. They were fair questions to ask, but answering them was a complex issue for me. If I told on the bully seniors, I would definitely pay for it later. If I stood my ground and made it about me, I would get into trouble with the principal. I chose the principal's office. How bad could it be? My mother had always submitted a document to be kept in my student file that stated I could not be subjected to corporal punishment. My mother didn't allow hitting of any kind, including spankings, and most of the time that I was in trouble as a kid, it was for talking in class. Worst-case scenario in my head was that they would simply contact my mom. She would be mad at first, but then feel sorry for me once I told her the details. I knew I could plead my story to my mother so she didn't tell the principal about the bullies. Thoughts of finding another public school raced through my mind. It was a solid plan and was settled in my mind. I stood my ground.

The P.E. teacher didn't back down either. She was a bully herself, nearly physically forcing me to put on the uniform. The fated word spilled out of my mouth as she struck my legs with the horrendous, over-sized gym shorts. I called her a *bitch*. I was immediately issued a ticket to the principal's office. Even though this teacher had called me all sorts of names including spoiled brat, entitled prissy, among others, I was the one in the wrong. I was the teen and I was going to be punished. It was fine as long as I was getting out of *hell period*. Being expelled from this school altogether was another great idea surfacing in my head at this point.

I went to the office and the principal didn't bother looking into my file. I was paddled for every letter of the word *bitch*. It was the most excruciating pain I had ever felt in my life. When I was picked up from school that day, I didn't have to tell my mother what happened and in fact, I didn't want to tell her. I had allowed a corporal punishment to be brought against me and I thought it would upset my mother so much, I kept it to myself. In addition, I was embarrassed about being bullied. It made me feel stupid and weak as a person. At that time, bullying wasn't talked about as openly as it is today and most victims were silent.

As the days progressed, I proceeded to fake sick every single Thursday to get out of going to school. By Thursday, I couldn't stand the hallway terrorizations that I received from the majority of the people in the hall who hated me for no reason. Accidental bumps hurling me into lockers, horrible names shouted at me from down the hall, to the senior girls threatening to beat me after school is what I constantly endured. Being a small girl without any friends for back up was unbearable. I had never fought anybody. That wasn't my style. The sad thing is that I hadn't done one thing to these people besides *exist*.

Faking sick was an easy out when the going got too rough. My dad was a physician, and he could treat me at home if I was sick. I started using my mother's coffee from her coffee pot to dunk the mercury thermometer into in order to raise the temperature reading to fake a fever. It only took a couple of seconds and the thermometer reading would shoot to 104 Fahrenheit! I would also hold my hand around the coffee pot for a bit to conduct the heat to my hand and then I would place it on my forehead before walking into her bedroom with the thermometer in my mouth. This worked for a while until maybe she got smart about it and started retaking my temperature before school started. Well, as parents evolve, unfortunately so do kids. I soon figured out that if you simply shake a mercury thermometer the opposite direction, the mercury goes up and stays there. I don't feel bad for telling you this, as I know they don't sell mercury thermometers anymore and you shouldn't keep one around your house. Mercury thermometers are very dangerous and if you have one at your house, get rid of it! If you were to break it – especially by the methods described above, the mercury will get everywhere and is highly poisonous to you! This was an awesome trick for kids to fake sick in the 1980s, nonetheless.

Today, my daughter and I have joined a campaign to put an end (hopefully, one day) to bullying. Not only was I a victim of bullies (and still am on occasion), I witnessed others be physically bullied from the stronger kids (i.e.

athletes). I remember one day during recess in sixth grade, some of the football players grabbed a kid named Johnny and rammed his crotch downward, onto a 4-foot pole. I remember hearing later when Johnny returned to school after a hospital stay that Johnny would never be able to have children. I never understood what Johnny had done to these athletes? Nothing. He had done nothing but wear thick glasses and short pants.

Points to Ponder: If a kid is being bullied, they need to tell an adult, but I've seen statistics as low as only 1/3 of bullied children tell an adult. Kids need to know that there are ways to prevent bullying and make it stop without the kid's direct involvement. Those in authority cannot do anything about it if they do not know.

All parents should be very thorough when teaching their children about bullying and the consequences that might arise from their actions if they participate in bullying activities. Look for the signs that your child might be bullying others such as fighting, associating with aggressive friends, increased aggression, getting into trouble at school, ending up with new items or money (i.e. iPods, etc.).

As a parent, it is also suggested to look for the warning signs of bullying with your children such as unexplained injuries, lost items (i.e. iPods, lunch money, etc.), faking illness, and changes in eating, sleeping, declining grades and social avoidance, and decreased self-esteem.

CHAPTER 6 - THE SPARK

As time went on, I eventually picked up a couple of friends at the new high school. This made the bullying tolerable, but neither one of these girls could have physically defended me, nor would I have expected that. I was embarrassed even to talk about the subject of being bullied. I have such a strong personality; it was very difficult to admit weakness. I felt as though I was weak because people didn't like me and wanted to harm me. When I say that I made a couple of friends, I mean *two friends*. One of them, I only saw during one of my classes. The other, I only saw at lunch. I would panic while waiting for her each day by the cafeteria. The feeling of being alone and vulnerable was nearly more than I could stand. This was my new life. I had to live it. I have since rekindled the relationship with my friend Kerry and I find her to be an invaluable friend for life. This was my main friend during this time and I truly love her for life.

Eventually, my nightly long-distance phone calls with my DFW friends became less frequent. I had a long time boyfriend back in DFW that I had left behind without resolve. I shall call him Paul. We had been in puppy adoration since the fifth grade. I don't say love since I don't think we were capable of that in fifth grade. We were silly to think we would always be together, at least we eventually said that we would always be together the night of a family wedding that he attended with me. Not that I took him serious, as he was in the ninth grade and I was in the eighth grade at that time. However, given that we didn't even argue once and seemed to get along great, I was blind-sided with what eventually happened.

The night that my closest DFW friends turned on me will always be with me. As if things were not horrible enough in the new town, my best friends betrayed me. This was the first betrayal of many that I would get from people in my life and where my problem with trusting new people in my life surfaced. I had spent every single day of the summer with these girls, every lunch period; every intimate detail of my life was discussed with these *friends*. These were my very best friends, I considered them my sisters. However, I had moved away from them. They didn't consider me part of their sisterhood anymore. Kids can be so mean and heartless.

The house phone rang and I answered. On the other end, it was my group of friends, but they sounded different. Something was wrong and I could tell immediately. I heard Paul's voice in the background. There were also many other voices, some I didn't recognize. As they held the phone in the air, my best friends shouted out that Paul wanted to break up with me. Then, I could hear his voice as he asked another girl out (to date him) and as she giggled, she accepted his gracious offer. They all proceeded to laugh hysterically. They were having a great time. They came back on the phone with me, scoffed at me, asking me how it felt. This was callous and was the end of my phone calls and trips to DFW.

The following day after the incident, I received a random phone call from the girl's older sister (the girl that was now dating Paul). I answered the phone while standing in my parent's room so I was unable to talk back to this bully without my mother wanting to know what was happening. I pretended it was a friend from DFW. Again, the victim of a bully rarely wants to admit what is going on to an adult. Therefore, I listened to what she had to say. This girl told me who she was before insulting me, telling me her little sister was a better match for Paul, and threatened that if I ever came back to DFW, she was going to hurt me. She asked me if I was scared because 'I sounded scared' and so I said good-bye as if nothing was wrong and hung up the phone. Wow! I had just been bullied again by an older girl, but from where I used to consider my home. My heart was broken and I felt helpless. I was saddened by the loss of it all and didn't feel like eating. Not for a long time.

This spark commenced a life-long eating disorder. My body image distorted and I didn't see myself the same in the mirror. I felt obese at 100 pounds. At least in my head, that was what I saw as I looked at myself in the mirror. I had no appetite and when I did eat, I made myself throw up (i.e., bulimia). I threw up on a routine basis to the point as to where simply eating a bite would make me have the urge to vomit. This scared me, so I stopped inducing vomiting and switched my weight loss tactic to starvation (i.e., anorexia). I felt that I could be more attractive and people would accept me if I were skinnier. I lacked a self worth because I had never felt rejection. I felt ugly and didn't understand why Paul and my friends would do this to me. My disorder continued, but on occasion, I would feel hungry. I sneaked to the drug store, bought Dexatrim diet pills, and started taking them twice a day. This helped, but made me shaky. Actually, I felt horrible. The scales soon read 85 pounds and I became sickly in appearance, completely emaciated. My mom started to question me and eventually found my stash of diet pills. I made up a story that they were not mine; she flushed them down the toilet, and continued to nag me to eat. I persisted to pretend to be ill so I didn't have to go to school. This all worked out nicely.

Please realize, harming yourself in any way, including starvation, is never worth doing for absolutely *anything*. *You* are your best friend! A teen relationship is not serious. Believe me, 99.9% of the time, whomever you date in high school is not your life mate. The friends you make in middle school or even high school are probably not the friends you will end up having as an adult, as you will all disperse to different colleges around the country, create your own families, etc.

Even if you end up in a teen marriage, you are not mature enough as a teen to make a lifelong decision and will likely end up in divorce or worse, in an unhappy relationship *for life*. You have no idea who you will become as an adult. Likewise, as a married teen, you are clueless as to what your significant other will become as an adult.

I admit that I made up that statistic of 99.9%, but out of all of the lifelong friends that I have kept in touch with, none of them are still in a relationship with high school sweethearts. Take it upon yourself to enjoy high school relationships for what they are – life lessons and character builders. They are simply a collective learning experience. Don't start thinking long term with anybody. Spend plenty of time with your friends doing positive things and building lasting memories. Friends *can* be forever, as long as you tend to the fire and not let it go out. I didn't meet my very best friends until I was in my thirties. I consider these people to be family. As established adults, my husband and I fit in well with our friends and these are lifelong relationships. This goes to show you that you can always and will always meet new friends in life.

Committing to a teen relationship is probably one of the most common mistakes which most of the time; leads to poor decision making. Teens who think they are in love will do anything for their significant other, including self-sacrifices such as not going to class, not doing their homework, not applying for college, not putting themselves on a career path, etc.

Think about teen relationships this way and you can't go wrong: when you graduate, you are both going your separate ways to grow up into adults. For the moment, enjoy being teenagers. You both can maybe stay in touch via Facebook, Twitter, or whatever social media is popular, but you are not going to be together forever. Both of you will find your soul mates and maybe as adults, you can find each other again if it is meant to be. Committing to a lifelong relationship as a teen is committing under false pretenses. Don't do it! Now for the 1% of you who are in a healthy long-term relationship that began in high school – kudos to you, you've beaten the odds!

I pretty much continued with the eating disorder until my late twenties. I got to the point where I would pull over and run into a drug store to use their scale to weigh myself to see if I had gained weight throughout the day. I think that behavior is crazy, especially because I was a skin-covered skeleton. I look at pictures of me during this time and I look ill. Being this skinny is never attractive, it's quite the contrary. I loved cooking for others so I could experience the food without tasting it (a big symptom of an eating disorder). I existed on coffee, salad (mostly lettuce) with fat-free dressing and apples. Some days, it would be a couple of lettuce leaves and diet drinks. I was self-destructing and didn't know it.

Eventually, I was so malnourished; I was unable to chew on a bite of food. I went to the hospital emergency room where a doctor scared me into eating right. He said that any day, my hair would fall out, my heart would give out and I was on a road to death if I didn't stop starving myself immediately. If anything, my vanity took over. I took heed to the warning of my hair falling out, and I stopped starving. I couldn't just leave the hospital and stop at McDonalds for high calories, the doctor said that at the point my health was in, I had to be on calorie and nutrient controlled shakes. These were disgusting and I regretted ever starving myself every time I had to choke one down.

During my recovery, my husband took away my bathroom scales, thereby preventing me from obsessing about my daily weight fluctuations. When he later allowed me to have a scale in the bathroom, we made a deal that I wouldn't go under 110 pounds (I am only 5'1 tall). I still suffer from body image issues (dysmorphia), but I do control my anorexic tendencies. I don't like being hungry, nonetheless. I still get disgusted at myself looking in the mirror, even at 105 to 110 pounds. If I am 110 pounds, when I look into the mirror, I probably view myself at 130 pounds. I feel that it is something that I will have to psychologically fight forever. Whatever, I like a good challenge. If I gain weight on occasion, I refer to it as being voluptuous. Voluptuous is much more attractive than bone skinny – at least for my body.

Points to Ponder: Adolescent friends are immature. Never take anything too seriously that your young friends do to you, even if it is hurtful. Realize that there are plenty more friends to be had and chances are, you'll meet your lifelong friends later in life.

Eating disorders are damaging to your body and do not solve anything for you – emotionally, physiologically, or physically. If you do not get help, you can do irreversible damage your body. You are your best friend and should treat your body with respect.

CHAPTER 7 - DEUTSCHLAND

When I was a sophomore, I met my daughter's father, a senior, at Nightmare High. I think I was open to being in a relationship after what had happened with Paul. Moreover, being in this new city and missing my old traitorous friends probably had me in an *off* mental state. I still wasn't eating very much when I started dating Whitney's dad. I was a virgin and didn't understand sex. I eventually gave in to it after being pressured every weekend for most of the school year. I hated it, didn't understand it and wished I didn't have to do it. Why did I do it? Because he was older and I was afraid of him leaving me for another, more experienced girl. I didn't want to be considered an immature baby. Wow, that line of thinking is so stupid! Why would I have thought that or even cared? After all, he was a senior and to me, he was a grown up, so he should know what is best. Yea, right!

Your virginity is something that is special and very dear to you. You only have it once, and once it is gone, it's gone. Take my advice and hold on to it as long as possible. Don't let others peer pressure you into thinking you should let it go. This is your choice and you should never allow someone; even if it's someone you believe you are in love with, to sway your decision! Pregnancy and / or sexually transmitted diseases are likely to arise – even on your first time with only one partner. Not to mention, your lifelong reputation is at stake if rumors get started. Avoid a mistake at all costs and think this very serious issue through before making a decision. The mistake could easily be a pregnancy that affects you for the rest of your life. The mistake could lead to a devastating disease that affects you for the rest of your life or worse, *ends* your life. On the other hand, at best, embarrasses the hell out of you when you have to visit the doctor!

Do me a favor: when and if you believe you are ready to give up your virginity, wait thirty days. If you both can agree, why not both be screened for STDs during this time? During this thirty day period, look at the person you are considering having sex with for the first time. You might be in love, but it is probably an infatuation. This will pass easily with time once you grow up. Picture this person fat with a balding head and a bad job. This could easily be your current loved one as an adult. How do you *know* you love him or her? You don't. As a teenager, you are too young! If at the end of thirty days, you still think it is right and you believe that s/he is worth the risk of pregnancy, disease &/or a degraded social status, then do what your heart tells you to do, but do it safely and use protection.

Enough of my rant on teenage sex. I'm obviously in a disagreement with the issue. I have the right to be because I made a mistake as a teen and became pregnant. I'm sure that many teens, hopefully older teens, are enjoying their sex lives without consequence because they are being smart and doing it safely. I want you at least to know my stance on it and maybe if I can extend the virginity of one teen in the world into their adult years, I've done my job. If you're an older reader who has moved past their teen years, maybe try to use this argument with the teens you come across with in life.

It was time to move to Europe. By this time, I had met another traitor-to-be, we shall call her Michelle. My friend Kerry and I were still great friends, but from what I recall, we had gotten into trouble quite often. I know around this time, I had a growing number of incidents with the Texas Alcohol Control Board for being a minor in possession of alcohol. My parents started grounding me from doing anything with Kerry and I can only guess that her mom didn't want her hanging out with me, either. However, I was the ringleader and I was the bad influence – not her. My parents should have grounded me from myself, if that were possible. I hope that Kerry and I, now that I am a law-abiding citizen, can make more happy memories in the future. I miss her.

Michelle was a new friend that I soon considered my best friend and my third friend I had made at Nightmare High. I think that is a curse, actually. In my life, most of the people that I considered a *best* friend eventually ended up backstabbing me. Today, I just have *good* friends and my daughter Whitney is my best girl friend for life.

To my delight, my parents offered me a deal that I could take anybody I wanted with me to Germany to live for a semester. I think they saw how hard the move to Wichita Falls was and were afraid I'd go through the same slump again in a new school. Since most of my childhood DFW friends were out of my life and I only had one friend that I routinely hung out with, I chose Michelle and off to Germany we went.

Living in Germany as a colonel's daughter was an amazing experience. The people on the Air Force base treated me like royalty, giving a double salute to my car as we drove through the military base gates. I'm not proud of this, but once we figured out the military police protocol was to double salute the car, we'd have fun driving in and out of the gate, just to see how far we could take them. This was horrible behavior and believe me; I got a slap in the face from karma on a later date for how I treated these military guards at the gate. There is more to this story of karma when I talk about living as a dependent wife of an airman.

My parents elected to live off base in a small village called Bundenbach so we could get the real experience of living in Europe. It was no less than awesome to see how others lived in a country so far away. No central heat and air, the heaters were in the floor, and the toilet flushed the opposite way! At sixteen, we were of drinking age in Germany. This was a blast for teens that loved to party! My previously strict mother allowed us to have one drink when we'd go to the local pub in town since it was legal. The thing was, being a wealthy child, I always had plenty of money and we didn't stop at one drink. We were super good at hiding intoxication so nothing ever came of us having too many drinks at the pub.

The elder village residents didn't like Americans all too much for some reason. On occasion when I set out on adventures in the town and the surrounding forests, older women chased me with umbrellas shouting German while running after me, but I thought it was hysterical, nonetheless.

We traveled around Europe – seeing the shows, shopping, visiting the monuments and enjoying the various cultures and traditions. We had an absolute blast, but it was the end of the semester before I could blink an eye. Michelle was going to go home to Texas and I'd lose my best friend, my roommate, my sister. Michelle and I were the closest that two friends could be and we spent every minute together. We had fun making silly videos, cooking, going on nature hunts, flirting with German boys, and even catching bees and writing songs about them.

In addition, I knew that being alone in Germany would make me miss Whitney's dad-to-be even more. I had been writing to him often and was heartbroken for having to leave him to go to Germany. The feminine vultures in the armpit were already trying to claim my spot with him only days before I left town. Being around Michelle got him off my mind, but I knew I'd sink into sadness once she left. Especially living in a village away from the military base where I could potentially make other friends from school. This was before the internet and cell phones and it wasn't as easy to combat loneliness as a teen.

I made a huge push to move back with Michelle for the next semester. The friends we had jointly made at the high school on the military base were great, but they lived thirty minutes away and I'd be living in the German boonies. We didn't even have American television and were stuck watching VHS tapes for entertainment. Given the past circumstances, my parents finally agreed to one semester in Texas and then my senior year would be Europe by myself. I agreed. I was going back to Texas.

In my new living arrangements, I'd have to share a bedroom with Michelle, but this would be all right. Even though we had our own space at my three-story Germany house, Michelle and I had never fought, so I figured it would be fine. At this point in my life, I had never lived in a small house. I always had anything I wanted, the moment I asked for it.

My life was about to change drastically. Little did I know that it was a disaster in the making!

Points to Ponder: Keep your virginity as long as you can. There's only one person to give it to and there's nothing more awesome than giving it to someone special on your wedding night. Strive for that! Don't focus on teenage relationships, live your teenage years as a teenager.

As far as friends go during high school, take them at face value for what they are. You are far too immature always to do the right thing by each other and kids always make mistakes. In my opinion, a teen's best friends should always be their parents.

CHAPTER 8 - TROUBLED TEEN IN TEXAS

Living in Texas with Michelle, her older brother, and her single mother was an experience that I'd love to forget. In my opinion, it was the strangest experience of a family life that I'd ever witnessed. I didn't see this side of her family before when I lived in Texas with my parents. Probably because Michelle usually hung out around our house and I found out exactly why.

It was a tiny house for four people to live in, to say the least. I could add more details for shock value, but I don't think they contribute to my story so I will omit and move on – no sense in dwelling on the negative. The pantry was bare for the most part and the refrigerator was the same. Michelle's mom didn't cook much at all. This was when I began to realize that not everybody in the country lived as well as I had during my childhood.

I ate at school during lunch. The living conditions did not matter because Michelle was my friend and we were going to have fun. However, the lesson learned from this experience is that on the surface, people might appear one way, but in real life, they might be different. Don't ship your kids to live with someone across the globe until you've had them checked out thoroughly!

Michelle and I agreed before leaving Germany that I would be allowed to go on a date once per week with my boyfriend, Whitney's father-to-be. Michelle had a crush on a boy and had plans of making a weekly date night the same night that I would go on a date. This didn't pan out for Michelle and soon, the fights over me hanging out with Whitney's dad-to-be commenced. Even though she was from the town, Michelle didn't seem to have any other friends to hang out with at Nightmare High. She started going on rants in front of me with her mother against my date nights. It was uncomfortable and very strange.

The fights began because Michelle didn't have a date on our agreed upon date night and I still wanted to go out with Whitney's dad-to-be. Seven days of the week and I was allowed *one* night to date and this was now being disputed. Wow, it didn't seem so unreasonable. Hindsight is great; I probably should not have gone out with him as it ended up being a bad decision. At the time, nobody could have told me differently. I wished I had this book when I was a teen, written by my future self. I don't regret Whitney, but it would have been much better to have her later in life – not when I was barely eighteen years old.

Unexpectedly, I started to feel ill on a daily basis. Cigarettes tasted horrible, I attempted a sip of alcohol, and it made me throw up. My breasts were tender and my body was changing. My brother had transferred colleges from TCU (in Ft. Worth) to MSU (in Wichita Falls), so he lived in the same town. I started hanging around my brother and his girlfriend more so I could get away from Michelle's mother who at that time was rude when I'd see her. My brother Eric and I had always been quite close. He was five years older than I was so at this time, he was 22 years old.

He played soccer for MSU in addition to his classes and was quite busy. This is probably why my parents allowed me to go back to Texas for a semester – they had Eric watching over me and knew he'd be there for me if I needed him. They were right.

My brother's girlfriend, upon hearing how I was feeling, took me to the clinic for a pregnancy test. Sure enough, the test was positive. I was scared and devastated. I didn't fully understand the ramifications of what had happened. We told Eric immediately and he started making sure that I was eating properly and had everything I needed. We had a plan in action and I had only a month and a half left in school to get through before I moved back to Germany. I told Michelle the news. I told her I'd be going to my brother's apartment after school that day. I needed to, as they were helping me get everything on track with my pregnancy.

An unexpected knock on the door sounded. It was Michelle. She had all of my items packaged up in a box and put them on the floor as I opened the door. She walked away, out of my life forever, without saying a word. I saw her at school, but she wouldn't speak to me. The traitor had surfaced. I needed a best friend as this was a difficult time in my life, being seventeen and pregnant - with my parents across the globe. She completely turned her back on me. It was more than upsetting to see that I found myself alone. I only had my brother who was busy with athletics and school. I didn't have a friend my age to talk to and my parents were across the globe.

I suppose being pregnant at seventeen meant that I couldn't do anything fun with Michelle anymore. Maybe it was because she had used me for all it was worth and with me being pregnant; she didn't see a use for me in her life? Whatever it was, we both have lasting memories of a great friendship that can never be discussed. We lived in Europe together, spent every day together for nearly a year and were as close as sisters could be. It's simply sad. I wished she had continued to be in my life. Nevertheless, I can honestly say that given the situation, I don't want her in my life. I wish the best for her, but life is too short to surround yourself with people that have the capacity to turn their back on you in a time of need.

Points to Ponder: Never change the path of your life for a relationship, especially as a teenager. Most of the time, the only people who truly have your back in life are your family - and in some families, there might be exceptions to that.

Keep the channels of communication strong between parent and child. If the parent to child bond is strong enough, the child is less likely to turn to friends or puppy love relationships and make the wrong decisions.

CHAPTER 9 - NEWS FROM ACROSS THE GLOBE

When I was two months pregnant, it was time to travel back to Germany. I was leaving my brother's protective wings and at that time, he was the only adult in my family that knew what I was going through. Honestly, what does a typical young guy know about being pregnant? Nothing.

I took my seat on the plane next to a mother and her toddler. The hyperactive child was two-years old and for the entire twelve-hour flight, she climbed on me, took my soda and peanuts, and irritated the living hell out of me. I had never been around a child before. Maybe a younger sibling of one of my friends for a minute, but I had managed in my life thus far to avoid all interaction with anybody under five years old. Being the baby of the family had its benefits, I supposed.

My parents picked me up at the airport in Germany. I wore my baggiest attire as not to let them realize I had a growing bump in my tiny belly. I'm barely five foot 1 inch tall and very petite. Back then, I was entirely too skinny and any weight gain would have been apparent. My brother had stepped up my dietary regimen, but I was still very thin.

I knew I didn't have long before it was obvious what was physiologically going on with me. However, my mother was very naïve and would never in a million years have thought that I would have had sex and much less become pregnant. She still lived in the fifties when kids were pure and innocent for the most part. Teen pregnancy just didn't happen. On the other hand, if it did, nobody spoke about it.

The next thirty or so days of my life were the longest, most stressful days I had lived thus far. I wanted to tell her about the pregnancy, but I knew that she would not have understood. I thought she would believe I was a demon, a horrible person. She already knew that I dabbled with alcohol and cigarettes, so I didn't want to disappoint her further. You may wonder why I do not speak of my father regarding this issue. Well, he wasn't the actual *parent* in my situation. As I said before, he was a lovable surgeon who worked very hard to support his family. Because of that, he was not the disciplinarian. I thought it was great that he was like that when I was a kid, but now I do feel sorry for my mom having to be the heavy.

Finally, my mother asked me, "Do you need me to get you some tampons?"

I replied abruptly while avoiding eye contact, "No."

She countered, "But you've been home over a month and you don't need any? Are you still having periods?"

I replied solemnly while hanging my head low, "No."

She continued in an anxious tone, "We were not in Texas doing what married people do, were we?"

Humiliation ensued. I wanted to crawl into a hole and die. I ran off to my bedroom to hide. At this point, she already knew that I was pregnant. I found out later that my mother had just received a letter from Michelle's mother only a few days prior, which was filled with hysterical stories. I can only assume that Michelle's mother was making sure that she would not receive blame for anything that had transpired with me, so she painted this horrible picture of what had happened while I was in Texas. I could be quite snarky given a few facts here, but again, I'll keep it to myself since it doesn't contribute to the overall picture of how I eventually earned a PhD. Taking the high road is a very difficult thing to do, believe me.

After a night of hiding under the covers of my bed and my mother pacing the hallway, she finally calmed down and sat next to me in my bed.

"I'll support you in whatever you decide to do," she said.

"I'm having the baby," I countered with a whimper.

Then, the next thing shocked me. She said, "Well, have you picked out a name yet?"

Acceptance. The pregnancy was finally accepted by her. This was the moment that I had struggled with for the three months of knowing I was pregnant. This moment had finally come and I sighed away three months of tension.

Telling my father was easy; he always went with the flow. He might have spouted out a few sentences of wisdom, but he remained *kid friendly*. He was the good guy in any situation.

After speaking about the situation in length, my mother decided that it was not appropriate for me to continue my education at the military base. It might have been because my father was a colonel, the highest ranked officer on this base (there were no General's stationed at the base at that time), and it would have appeared inappropriate for his daughter to be an unwed, pregnant teenager. Whatever the reason, I would have to drop out of school no matter what I decided to do, move back to the armpit, and be with

Whitney's father. Alternatively, I could have stayed in Germany and lived at home, not furthering my education and simply existing.

The best decision I could have made would have been to stay in Germany. At seventeen, I needed loving parents. My dad was a doctor, my mother a nurse, and both could have taken the best care of me during the pregnancy. At seventeen, I didn't know what was good for me, who was good for me, or how to plan my future. This was a mistake. This was a huge catastrophe about to happen. I decided to move back to the armpit for the third time. I'm not sure how it all happened, but we decided to get married.

Points to Ponder: When it comes to pregnancy and your health, complete honesty is always best – it ultimately cannot be avoided, so do not allow time to pass without receiving adequate medical care. In addition, the stress of keeping the secret can itself be harmful to you and the baby.

As a teen, if you act as an adult, such as by electing to have sex, realize that you may have to continue acting as an adult when your actions land you with lifelong consequences such as pregnancy or disease. Do not engage in adult activity unless you are prepared to end your childhood and forever be a grown-up.

CHAPTER 10 - THE OMEN

I find myself, seventeen and pregnant, in a small dressing room of a maternity store. I had never stepped into a maternity store before or even seen maternity clothes. In the eighties, maternity clothes were neither stylish nor cute - especially for a teenager. This was my own personal hell. I had traded in my micro miniskirts for frumpy dresses and one-piece jump suits.

At 5 foot 1 inch tall, not a dress in the store fit me. I believe I might have tried on a hundred dresses that day, my mother eventually handing me every dress in the store in a size small. Everything looked horrible and appeared to be ten sizes too big. I might as well have worn huge sheets with a neck hole cut out. We changed stores and the fitting room nightmare continued. My luck didn't change until the final dress of the day. It was black, but it looked the least disastrous. Maybe I just gave up and gave in? Little did I realize through the tired, hormonal haze that I had just purchased a black maternity wedding dress to be worn in the justice of the peace's office where I would wed, as a minor, a nineteen-year old college student. I know my parents had to be proud. That last sentence was riddled with sarcasm, obviously. My mother had flown in from Germany to attend this horrendous ceremony. Of course she did! I was only seventeen and wasn't old enough to consent to marriage. She had to sign me away to this other teenager. Great. There is a reason why minors can't engage in a contract.

The black maternity wedding dress was probably a stern sign, or more like an *omen*. I think with this many odds stacked against this relationship, what happened in the end was fated.

At seventeen, I was married and living with my in-laws in the bedroom that my new teenage husband grew up in as a child. Weird? Yes. My parents were to be in Europe for the next two years. I would have to go this pregnancy alone, without my parents. At least my brother was in town and I had some form of sanity to lean on when I needed him.

I should mention that in my opinion, I didn't have an overall positive relationship with my in-laws. I can write another book on that relationship on another day if I feel like writing a non-fiction horror story. I'm going to leave this one alone for the sake of my daughter, per her request. To give an overview, at seventeen and pregnant, I didn't feel any emotional support from this family.

My biggest surprise was having a daughter. The entire pregnancy was riddled with predictions from wanna be voodoo magicians saying it was a boy because I was carrying the baby low or because a pencil turned one way and whatever other ludicrous jinx BS people threw at me. Nobody cared to discuss girl names with me so I decided to name her Whitney, after the late Whitney Houston who was one of the most talented artists during that time. I was laughed at for selecting the name (Whitney Whatley), and ridiculed because it rhymed. I liked it, thought it sounded cute. I figured it sounded like a great name for a cheerleader or an actress – either or both was what I wanted Whitney to be one day. Thus far, she has been a two-time state champion cheerleader and we are about to start looking for our first movie roles. Our fingers are crossed that we can score some roles eventually.

The day that my water broke, I told my teenage husband it was breaking and he replied that I was urinating on myself and he left for his college classes. I hadn't urinated on myself previously so there was no precedence for this evaluation. I sat in the middle of the living room floor, waiting, timing my contractions. On this day, I was one week overdue with the pregnancy due date. Go figure. Unaware of what I should do, I sat for four hours while I waited for him to return. This was the pre-cell phone era so when you were out, you were unavailable. I found out later that I could have spawned an infection from the water breakage, but of course, my parents were in Europe and would have been the ones to know this and rush me to the hospital. I finally called my obstetrician after four hours and he instructed me to rush to the delivery room immediately.

As I was getting ready to leave, my teenage husband drove up and I waddled into the car with him to journey to the hospital on the icy roads. Once we arrived at the hospital, we drove around for a spell looking for a parking lot. As teenagers, we didn't know what an emergency entrance of a hospital looked like or did we have a clue that I should've been dropped off at one. In labor, I traipsed across the icy parking lot and ambled into the hospital foyer. We climbed a few flights of stairs and located the delivery suite. As teenagers, we didn't always look for such things like an elevator or think to ask the hospital staff what we should do or where we should go.

Other than the actual birth of my daughter, my fondest memories of this day are when my brother arrived with a huge box of chocolates in hand, after my epidural anesthesia was in place. As I sat in the bed, with contractions rising, a chocolate fight ensued. My brother and I laughed hysterically as the monitor notified me that I was having contractions. I think my brother was scared for me so he threw chocolates at me to get our minds off what was really happening. I, of course, threw them right back across the room. Scary thing - I was about to be a parent. I never said I was mature and at that time, I was only a kid. The nurse finally came in and told me it was time to deliver. Epidurals are awesome; I never realized it was time.

After about five minutes, Whitney arrived and the biggest surprise was when the doctor said *it's a girl*. I couldn't believe it, I was so happy. Not knowing the sex of the child was like the ultimate Christmas present. This emotion can never be replaced or duplicated (unless I had another child, of course). Whitney was so beautiful and healthy at 8.4 pounds. The looming problem was that my eighteenth birthday had just passed and I had never been around a kid under five years old. I *needed* a girl at this stage of my life; I thought I would know what to do for a girl. The nurse had to instruct me how to hold Whitney for the first time. In my arms, a smile plastered across my face as I held my new lifelong best friend.

The in-law troupe immediately left the hospital to celebrate with my teenage husband and this was the first moment in this endeavor that I felt real pain. The epidural had worn off and I climbed the rails of the hospital bed. My brother was still there to comfort me, but he eventually had to leave to go to class. The nurse arrived, asking me to name my beautiful baby girl. I surveyed the room. I was alone. Nobody was there to share this with me. I responded, *Whitney*. I won. I named her what I wanted to name her and nobody was there to say anything different. I explained to the nurse that I'd save the middle name for my teenage husband to choose later. I had toyed with Olivia, O. and other names starting with the letter o in attempt to make her initials W.O.W. but just couldn't decide on any of those names. I was a teenager, don't judge. The initials W.O.W. would have been cool...at least to me.

I had just become a teenage mother and a high school dropout. I had no friends. I was married at seventeen to another teenager. I was living in Texas in my in-law's home with my parents across the globe in Europe. I had no emotional support besides that from my brother. My future was bleak.

Points to Ponder: The day that you or your significant other become pregnant, read an entire book about pregnancy and become informed about everything. Go to the hospital in advance and map out your plan for the big day. Discuss your pregnancy thoroughly with your doctor and leave no question unanswered.

CHAPTER 11 – DEVASTATION TO MOTIVATION

I surveyed my life after the next couple of months. It was time to get out of that house before I lost my sanity. My teenage husband quickly ended his college career and got a job - a job about as lucrative as a teenager would be able to get at that time, in that town. We applied for government-subsidized housing and were accepted. My first adult home on my own was a government-subsidized apartment – certainly no white picket fences here. However, who really wants a white picket fence, anyway? I mean, seriously, I find them tacky. I digress.

The two-bedroom apartment cost us $104.00 per month and even this was a financial strain. Every time we turned on the light, hundreds of roaches scurried into the crevices. I had never seen a roach before and now I was roommates with thousands of them. Scorpions also infested the tattered apartment complex and I would occasionally dodge one as I walked on the sidewalk. One time, in my apartment, I was stung on the arm by one as I was getting dressed. The scorpion had crawled into my shirt that I had put on my chair the night before. Gross, right? By the way, being stung by a scorpion feels like someone is poking a shard of glass into your skin. Ouch! Because of the infestation, Whitney was never allowed to crawl on the floor. The carpet was void of padding and ripped away at the edges of the rooms, exposing the concrete. This definitely wasn't what I expected to live in as my first home. This was an absolute nightmare. I had plummeted from a stately family home in the wealthiest town per capita in Texas (Westover Hills) to a government-subsidized, worn down apartment where I once heard a gunshot ringing from a distance in the complex and routinely listened to screaming from my dysfunctional neighbors.

Being a high school dropout at eighteen with a child to take care of was a major thorn in the side of my career. I searched the want ads in the newspaper for a job. I wasn't qualified for any of the jobs. I had always been interested in cosmetology – what girl wasn't? Therefore, it seemed plausible to look into beauty colleges. It seemed to be a perfect fit for my situation, as they didn't require a high school diploma. I found out that I would qualify for a government loan for the one-year program. The plan was born. I would become a licensed cosmetologist.

As I prepared to start school, I found myself in a situation with very limited clothing and a miniscule budget. I didn't have the means to purchase clothing to wear to school. My teenage husband and I were adamant about only accepting minimal support from my parents, as we wanted to prove we could support our family. This was not a good decision and we should have accepted more help – we needed it!

It would have been silly for me to continue wearing baggy maternity clothes, but I really didn't have a choice. I had gone from a fashion snob to a fashion disaster. To my relief, upon admittance into Aladdin Beauty College, they assigned me a couple of smocks that I was supposed to wear every day. I simply wore the smock with a bra under it and a rolled up pair of my baggy maternity sweats to school. Whatever worked was fine with me. I no longer cared what my clothing looked like - I had bigger fish to fry.

My parents sent me a monthly check to help with the baby and other living expenses. We eventually purchased a $600 dollar car for me to drive. This was a massive downgrade from what I drove as a younger teen, but at least I had wheels. However, the ones assisting me with the early care of my daughter had urged me not to breastfeed, which would have been healthier for Whitney and of course, less expensive. I didn't know how to breastfeed on my own, so I had to go with the advice of my elders. This was yet another casualty of my parents being in Europe and another reason why I should have never left Germany after my parents found out that I was pregnant.

I had to purchase expensive baby milk formula and that was draining our limited budget – not to mention the disposable diapers, accessories, and clothes for my baby girl. I was barely eighteen at that time, and in my mind that translated to about fifteen years of age. I was a slow developer as far as maturity goes. Intelligent, but immature. I like to refer to myself as a *Peter Pan*. That's a much nicer term and since I love to dress up in costumes, it fits.

The first day of beauty school, I dropped Whitney off at the daycare. I was surprised to see a somewhat familiar face. Her name was Dina and she was one of my husband's classmates from high school. She was one of the few older girls at Nightmare High that was ever friendly to me, so I was glad that she would be taking care of my newborn. She told me that she had a newborn too. Her name was Shalah, and she became Whitney's lifelong best friend. I felt exhilarated as I drove to beauty school for my first day. Dina and I became fast friends and she later was my maid of honor in my wedding. I love Dina to this day and thank her for finally allowing me to have a friend to count on in my life. She was the first dear friend that I had made since high school and I desperately needed a peer at that time, especially one with a child that would understand what I was going through in life.

I hadn't smoked cigarettes since I found out that I was pregnant, but I walked into the beauty college and confronted a cloud of smoke rising from the break room. Well, if you can't beat them, join them. I started smoking cigarettes again, as it was a social ritual to sit and chat with the other beauty students during breaks. I confined my habit to school, spending the little tip money I earned at school from the patrons on my cigarette habit.

I graduated in the minimal time of nine months and my parents, still in Europe, told me over the phone that they were so proud of me for graduating beauty school. I suppose I was pleased too and ready to start my career and make all of the money that the school's recruiter told me would be waiting for me as soon as I started working in the field. Just a side note: recruiters always embellish with the best possible scenarios to encourage you to sign up and pay for their program. I'm not calling them liars, but they don't exactly recruit you by telling you it will be very hard to make a living at first after you graduate from their school. Always take what they say with a grain of salt, if you know what I'm saying.

About this time, my husband (Whitney's biological dad) came home from work one day and told me that he wanted a divorce. I was shocked. I assumed that he probably had his eyes on another woman. We didn't have a luscious life or anything, how happy could he have been? I was hysterical, cried all night. Maybe this was the second or third time I had cried in my life – not counting my newborn years when I didn't have much self-control. My tears do not flow freely, by the way. Some, including my mother, consider me void of all forms of emotion except happiness and rage. My parents were still in Europe and I was alone in the States with the exception of my brother who was busy with soccer and school.

The thought of divorce frightened me. I had never been out on my own, much less with a baby to take care of all by myself. I was only eighteen and very embarrassed to talk about the situation with my family. Looking back on the past, I should have called my parents in Germany for a ticket home and let him have his way out of our teenage marriage. The details are blurry in my mind about these few days. Somehow, we worked it out and decided to stay together and not get divorced. However, this day marked the day that I began to fall out of puppy love with my teenage husband. Each day over the next year, I woke up feeling less and less in love with him. It might have taken over a year to solidify the loss of feelings, but it eventually happened. When I finally woke up, I realized I had never been in love.

After deciding not to get divorced, Whitney's father and I eventually bought a $30,000.00 house together. I think I agreed to this because I was growing very unhappy in the marriage and thought that buying a house would give me a much needed distraction. I also wanted Whitney to have more room. We couldn't afford much, as we were both in entry-level jobs. The small house smelled like propane gas and it most likely had thirty coats of paint on the walls. It definitely wasn't my dream house.

I had grown up watching two parents in love, without arguments, in a stable relationship. I figured that once you were married, you were married. I didn't understand the fighting aspect of marriage. That wasn't supposed to happen. I had never seen this example, so I knew something wasn't right with this relationship. I wanted better for Whitney. The hurt of rejection that I felt the day he asked me for a divorce burned inside of my soul, later consuming me as I started to despise him, wanting nothing more than to get away. It just wasn't the right time to break free.

I took my first job as a hair stylist at a major chain salon at the mall. The manager had an authority complex and was very aggressive. She loved her reign over her employees. She would shout orders just to hear herself talk and because she could. If towels were already cleaned and folded, she would have you refold them just so you wouldn't sit around. This seemed very excessive and hard hitting to me. I didn't like authority as it was, but she really pushed it with me. I had grown to be a good hair stylist and nail technician. After a while, I started getting regular clients and eventually, I was booked out for the month. I enjoyed the camaraderie with the other stylists and besides the manager; it was a fun job to have.

Then, the fated day arrived. One of my male clients came in for his normal cut and style. This was the day that an ember flamed in my mind, and I decided to go to college. As I was cutting my client's hair, he made small talk with me.

He asked bluntly, "What are you in school for?"

I was baffled as thoughts flooded through my confused mind - *What does he mean? I went to school for this, for what I'm doing?*

After a brief delay, I finally answered with a question, "What do you mean?"

He continued boldly, "What are you going to do as a career?"

Wow. I thought what I was doing was my career. I felt stupid. Like I was settling for something. It was as if working at the salon wasn't a career that I could be proud of for some reason.

I must say this now; I think that being a hair stylist is a great career with the same upward mobility as just about any career that's out there with the exception of post secondary degrees (i.e. M.D., PhD, etc.). I think it is fun, creative and can be quite lucrative when you work your way to the top of the industry. However, this client sparked something in my brain that day that being a stylist was looked upon as a stepping-stone to something better – at least for me. Maybe he just detected something else inside of me that was bursting to come free? I was impressionable and took it to heart. I met with a college advisor immediately.

Points to Ponder: In my opinion, if your spouse asks for a divorce and is completely serious about it, if you can muster the strength and support yourself, grant it immediately. Asking for a divorce is a momentous issue and should be treated seriously. This person is declaring that they are willing to separate from you permanently. I believe in most situations, there's something going on bigger than you know and you need to move on with your life. I don't think that you should waste valuable time and stay together for the sake of the children, as I think it does more emotional harm than good.

CHAPTER 12 - BEAUTY CAREER DROP OUT

I learned from meeting with the college advisor that I had to take the GED (General Education Degree) exam prior to my admission and if I passed, this would be considered a high school diploma equivalent. This was my first step toward college. As long as I could pass the exam, I would be able to start the process to get into college. I was very nervous to take the exam, but I wasn't going to be surprised if I failed, as I had been a failure on purpose during my years of high school. I went to the exam with a nonchalant attitude and surprised myself when I ended up scoring a 100%.

I quit my job at the hair salon and paid an agency to find me a job in a medical office. I wanted to be in the medical field because I had grown up working in my dad's clinic every summer and was interested in the medical field. At this time, I wanted to be a registered nurse like my mother and I wanted to get experience in the medical field. With the experience that I had gained from my father's clinic, I believed I had experience and could work as a medical receptionist. For a $5.00 an hour job, I paid this agency

$1000.00 to help me get the interview. They took the money directly out of my paychecks so I didn't have an income for over a month. Even with experience, it would have been difficult to land a job in the medical field at my age, especially without a high school diploma. When you are starting out in the world, sometimes it is best to take your hits. I've never found that an immediate reward is worth it in the end.

I made a friend, a fellow medical receptionist at the medical office where I landed my first medical job. She had an MS degree in psychology and was finishing her PhD in psychology. She needed to administer standardized IQ (Intelligence Quotient) tests to a number of people for her dissertation. I agreed to help her out and so I signed up to take the IQ test. It was very long, boring, and after half of it was over, I wished that I had lied and told her that I couldn't find a babysitter.

She finally reported to me at work one day about a week later that I had scored a 139. I had no idea what that meant. I was embarrassed and told her not to tell anybody. She proceeded to tell me that I was a point away from being a genius. I thought a few times that I should have tried a little harder and not skipped some questions because I was bored. Maybe I could have earned the title of genius? Maybe one day, I will retest? And maybe not.

Knowing for the first time in my life since middle school that I was smart gave me the second spark that I needed to push my way into college. Even with an average IQ, anybody can get into college the way that I did and anybody can complete a degree. What your major is might vary, but there are programs for anybody willing to put the hard work into it.

My advice is *not* to have your IQ tested. I simply stumbled upon the test and acquired my intelligence ranking and this helped me, but I strongly advise you that this was a huge risk. Had the test gone the other way and I would have found that I was average or even below average, it would have zapped all of my self-esteem with academics. I might not have gone to school. I thereby advise against knowing how smart you are until you are out of school. You will fit into the classes you are designed to be in by interest alone. If math and science are difficult for you, shoot for something else that interests you like journalism, language, art or music. There is something for everybody.

With my GED in hand, I went back to the advising office. They signed me up for the ACT (American College Testing - college entrance exam). This exam includes tests for English, math, reading and science. There is also an optional writing exam. I took the exam and did very well, especially on the writing section. That surprised me, I had no idea that I was good at writing, but at this point in my life, I wasn't good at anything academic. I didn't take the SAT (Scholastic Aptitude Test) as my old classmates did. I didn't even go to school my senior year of high school.

I sauntered into the financial aid office of the university. I had a friend that received a government grant that paid for her living expenses, tuition, books and even some daycare. She had a few kids, but that was an awesome deal. Please note, there are more financial aid opportunities for young mothers than there were back in 1990. Not only can you receive financial aid in the form of loans, you can also receive grants from the government that you do not have to pay back. You do not have to start paying on your loans until about six months after you get out of school!

Here is the problem that I encountered. My parents claimed me on their taxes and therefore, I had to show proof of their income in order to qualify for a federal grant.

I was a 20-year-old mother, high school dropout, but because my dad was a doctor and made too much money, it made me ineligible for the grant. Fair enough. Mom and Dad had to pay cash for my college. I have heard that the new rule is that if you are 24 years old or above, you don't need your parent's income documents and can apply on your own. Good to know. For those of you who do not have parents to pay for your school, never use that as an excuse. If you did well in high school, you are eligible to apply for scholarships. There are *always* academic scholarships available that I was told before go unused each semester. The one time I applied for one, I received it! Why didn't I continue to apply? I didn't want to take from others that really needed it; I learned this concept from my parents. My mother was bored in Germany but didn't take a job on the base because it would take from someone who needed it, so she simply volunteered at the hospital.

Even if you didn't do that good in high school, it isn't over for you. If you can test into a college with your ACT, you are still eligible for a student loan or grant. Say that you don't test well enough on your ACT. Guess what? It's still not over for you! Go to your local community college and see what they have to offer you. You can take your basic courses here (i.e. math, English, etc.) and when you are ready, you can take the ACT and transfer your credits to a four-year university. The diploma is the exact same if you started in a community college or started at the university. As long as you are there your final two years (this may differ per university so check before you go on my advice here), you will receive the diploma with the school's name on it. In addition, this is inevitably a cheaper route.

Either way, if you do university or community college, park your booty in the financial aid office and demand to know every single option that is available to you and don't stop there. Whatever you decide to put down as your major (i.e. biology, journalism, film, music, etc.), stopover in the departmental office and ask if there are any scholarship opportunities available for newcomers. This can be free money! Don't pass up the opportunity for it because when you get in the real world, these free money opportunities go away for the most part. That is, unless you buy a lottery ticket, but you know the odds on winning that.

I was about to begin school at twenty years old, Whitney was two. I examined my feelings and realized that I didn't even have a flicker of love or romance left for my husband. He had hurt me so deeply the day he asked for a divorce unexpectedly. He had obviously been prepared to discard Whitney and I while my parents were still in Europe and Whitney was only 1 years old. I was done. When he came home that day, I told him that I wanted a divorce. It was time to live for my daughter and me. Moreover, my parents were due to move back to the United States and the timing was right. I was finally motivated to live for myself, get on track with a career that I could be proud of, and make a good living for my daughter's sake. I was ready to succeed by myself and for myself.

Points to Ponder: Everybody in this nation has the right and ability to attend school. Never make excuses for not getting an education. There's an academic fix for nearly any situation – including financial, disabilities, etc.

CHAPTER 13 - COLLEGE BOUND

My parents were both from southern Louisiana – my dad from New Orleans and my mom from Houma, which is south of New Orleans. They had raised their family, did their time in Europe, and were moving back to the States. My parents felt it was time to move back near the rest of their family. My parents urged me (along with Whitney) to move in with them as they moved to their new home. Moving locations hadn't worked out for me in the past and I was scared to make the change. I also didn't want to take Whitney away from her biological father because I grew up with two parents and felt that even though we were not together, it was the right thing to do. I thought she would blame me later if I moved her away. This was yet another big mistake. Whitney and I should have moved in with my parents. That would have been the best decision on all fronts.

My parents wanted me to focus on school so at this time, I didn't work while attending school full time. However, I had plenty of friends who were single with kids that worked jobs around their school schedule, so it definitely can be done. With my parents' financial help, I found an apartment for Whitney and myself. It was modest; to say the least, but a step above the government subsidy I had lived in immediately after she was born. I think my monthly rent was $280.00. It was one bedroom, not too far from the college (Midwestern State University), and I used my parent's stipend to purchase a waterbed from my friend and a television from a pawnshop. My friend that I had met in beauty college took me to some garage sales and I purchased other random furnishings. It was an eclectic place, but it was my home. It was the first home that I had as an adult on my own. The apartment didn't have padding under the carpet, but I was used to that. The walls were paper-thin and I could hear everything my neighbors did on a daily basis, but it was all that I could afford. At least the neighbors were not screaming at night like at the government-subsidized apartment and I never saw a roach in this place.

My dad gave me a pep talk and warned me that I was behind my peers by two years and that I would have to focus to keep up with them. I registered as a nursing major and started my first college classes, and it was more than exciting. Unfortunately, by this time, my brother had moved from Wichita Falls to join a band that was based in Austin, Texas. My brother is a child prodigy pianist and turned his skills on the ebonies & ivories to electronic keyboards. I was alone in this town, but at least Austin wasn't too far (i.e. 5 hour drive) and my parents had moved back to their home base in southern Louisiana (i.e. 10 hour drive). Dealing with a messy divorce in between study sessions and a crazed toddler that had a sleeping disorder was more than exhausting. Yes, my daughter Whitney had an adversity to sleep as a child. Wow, how things change! At this time, she might have passed out around midnight and was up with the sun. I had no choice but to study while she slept. I was a living zombie, but acclimated to the little sleep that I was able to capture. Maybe this contributed to my current insomnia.

My first semester, I ended up on the University Honor Roll. I was more than proud of myself going through a semester as a single parent, while enduring the hardships of divorce proceedings without family support in town. I tackled college level courses without a full high school education. I hadn't taken algebra, chemistry, or senior level English in high school as my peers had taken. Not only did I *maybe* have a D average at best with the three years of high school that I did attend, I didn't take many of the core classes. If you find yourself in this situation, it is not over for you!

In college, I took the remedial math courses since I was lacking in math education. I found the courses to be quite easy and even fun at times. Yes, it was an ultimate waste of time because the remedial courses didn't count toward a degree plan, but it was unavoidable. If your college advisor tells you to take these courses, you need to get over your pride and do what you have to do to get through it all and get on track. I love the saying that *Rome wasn't built in a day.* Your college education doesn't take a day, either. In a year, I was on track with anybody else who started with me and nobody knew the difference. Don't let that huge mountain deter you. Just put on your hiking boots and climb it. You'll feel so accomplished when you get the top!

What many people do not realize is that you can backdoor yourself into college by going the non-traditional route as I did. Even without a high school diploma, if you list yourself as a non-traditional student on your application, (non-traditional means that you are not applying straight out of high school), you don't have the same restrictions as your peers did when they came straight out of their senior year of high school. The top 10% rule for admission won't apply to you as it would if you were applying as a high school senior. If your high school grades are not good enough to get into a university, do what I said before and go to a community college first. You'll need to prove yourself and then backdoor your way into a university within a year or two. Where there is determination and desire to achieve, there is always a way around things.

Whitney's third birthday was around the corner and I looked back with fond memories about my early dance classes and recitals. I searched for the best dance studio in town and found my new future family at Studio 5,6,7,8. Not only did I register Whitney for her first dance class, but I also registered myself for a class with my age girls. I talked my friend Dina into signing up Shalah (Whitney's BFF) for the same classes. In no time, I landed a job at the studio as a dance teacher. Soon after, I auditioned for and became a member of a competitive dance group. Whitney's number of dance and gymnastics classes soon rose into the double digits. The dance studio became a home away from home for both of us.

I met a few friends during college, but I called them party friends. These were the kind of girls who would leave you at a nightclub if they met a guy and went home with him – leaving you stranded without a ride home. Please use my rule of thumb and do not date anybody you meet in a nightclub. Do you really want to tell your kids and everybody you ever meet that asks how you met your significant other that you met them in a nightclub? Probably wouldn't be your first choice, right? Not to say that you cannot find true romance in a smoke filled pickup joint, but why don't you save the *love at first sight* moment for a library, a class, a dog park, or even the first day at work? In addition, going home with somebody you do not know is a very dangerous ritual. Not only do you not have time to get to know the person who might be a serial killer with AIDS, but also if you go missing, nobody knows where to begin to find you…*or your body.*

It seemed like each semester, I was cursed with a catastrophe that made it difficult to deal with my studies. Starting with the divorce during my first semester and working my way up to a furniture delivery guy stalker, it was a semester curse of which I was forced to deal.

Upgrading from the hand-me-down waterbed that had burst – probably due to Whitney jumping on it behind my back, I had ordered new bedroom furniture from a cheap furniture store that offered financing. They sent over a deliveryman that they probably did not run a criminal history check on. The creepy man set up my furniture and acted very strangely as he surveyed my apartment.

The next morning, he was back at my apartment, banging on the door. I saw him combing his straggly hair as I looked out the peephole. Being a smart woman, I remained silent and signaled Whitney to do the same. As we watched for him to drive away in his old beat up jalopy, we got on the phone with one of my friends and then immediately rushed over to her home. On the way to my car, an elderly neighbor said she had seen the same man delivering my furniture the day before. I asked her to remain watch at my apartment door and she agreed to do so as I rushed to my friend's house to come up with a plan.

A good friend of mine named Randy offered to stay at my place for the night while I stayed at another friend's house with Whitney – out of danger. He invited a few more of his friends to stay with him as back up. In the meantime, my elderly neighbor reported to me that the shady delivery man had come over two additional times and each time, he banged on my door with increasing valor and even stepped it up to peer into my windows. Randy arrived at my apartment with friends and beers in hand and prepared for the impending confrontation with the sinister furniture stalker. As expected, at 10 PM, the banging ensued on the door. Randy swung open the door and a verbal altercation commenced.

The trembling furniture stalker stammered, "I wasn't gonna hurt her or her little girl."

Strange, Whitney wasn't there when the man delivered my furniture. He had surveyed my apartment and figured out there were two of us and the other resident was a little girl. The furniture stalker explained that he didn't place the mirror piece on my dresser appropriately and he was coming back (all four times throughout the day) to put it on correctly. I'm thinking there is a very miniscule chance that he was the *employee of the year* at the cheap furniture store and cared about putting the shoddy furniture together correctly. The dresser was so second-rate; the mirror piece was designed simply to sit on top of the chest of drawers. There was nothing to install or set up inappropriately. Did this man think we were morons? I guess so. The stalker left the apartment abruptly after a heated exchange with Randy and all seemed to be solved as he traveled away in the darkness.

The next day, Randy sped off to the furniture store and demanded to speak to the owner. He explained what happened and the police were called to the scene. As the police arrived to the shifty furniture store, they called the furniture stalker by name as he had recently been released from jail. From what I recall, it was something to do with sexual assault and / or burglary. This man was fired on the spot by the storeowner, but that didn't help my cause. I had a convicted felon armed with my address and most likely pissed off at me for the loss of his job. It was time to move. I never slept another night in that place. The apartment office understood my dilemma and was gracious enough to let me out of my lease.

Not to bore you with the struggles that I called my semester curse, but let me make my point that when it seems too overwhelming or you think you've lost focus for the semester and just feel like dropping out, don't do it. Overcome the obstacles and say each time, *it builds character and makes me stronger.* You can sleep later, just get it done.

Points to Ponder: Life will throw hurdles at you along the way. Never allow an obstacle to throw you off course. Think of obstacles as challenges and celebrate when you win.

CHAPTER 14 - MEDICAL SCHOOL OR BUST

After making either the University Honor Roll and / or the Dean's List each semester, I decided to change my major. I had to talk to my parents first. My dad was the major academic and a previous pre-med major so I needed his advice. Since I had always pretended to be dumb in my teen years to get away with things, I knew I had some damage to undo with them. I had proven myself the previous year with good grades, but I hadn't yet reached my difficult courses yet and didn't know if my parents would take me seriously.

I was visiting my Uncle Frank and Aunt Norma's home in Jackson Mississippi with my parents and Whitney. It was Thanksgiving of 1991 when I told them I needed to talk about school. I explained that I wanted to change my major to pre-medicine and they were surprisingly receptive. It was the first time in my life since middle school that they must have realized that I wasn't an airhead.

After the holiday when I returned home, I rushed back to school to the Registrar's office and made the switch of my major. I sprinted over to the biology office and got a new degree plan on file. It was exciting. I scheduled a meeting with the pre-medical degree committee, which was made up of tenured professors in biology, chemistry and physics. My first meeting was disheartening. The committee was made up of older male professors. One of the members ended up being my organic chemistry professor the following semester. This man had the audacity to make an off the cuff remark that he believed women had a place in the kitchen, barefoot and pregnant, but if I wanted to try to make it in a man's world... go for it. I don't think today that with the social media the way it is, he would still have a job 24 hours after saying something like that to a young female student whether he was tenured or not! Nevertheless, who was I to tell on him? I wanted to get into medical school one day and making waves at the university wasn't going to get me there. He was tenured and I was a 21 year old undergraduate. Who would anybody believe or care about – him or me? I'd vote *him*, at least on that day, at that time.

I decided not to let it get to me and the first day of his organic chemistry course, he made a speech. He said that there would be one A, one B a handful of Cs, half the class would drop the course, and the rest would fail. He announced that the highest grade in the course would be mid-30s and therefore, we would all compete for the highest failing grade to get one of the coveted passing scores after he did the grade conversions. I set out to earn the honorary A in the course. I grabbed a study partner immediately, another female. With this professor, we had the odds stacked against us.

Organic chemistry was considered a weed-out course at the university, which meant that it would filter through only those students brave and smart enough to pass it and we would move on to the next year of undergraduate education in pre-medicine. MSU didn't want to release a bunch of ill-prepared pre-medicine majors out into the world, all applying and being rejected on their medical school applications. They only allowed their best applicants through. It was a very smart strategy if you are going after a 95%+ acceptance rate of the graduates from your program into medical school. That's a college recruiter's dream stat!

I poured every waking moment into studying and preparing for this course. Once, I attended class without preparing for his lecture and immediately was kicked out for not being able to answer a question. Whitney had been battling an ear infection and I had spent many hours in the emergency clinic the day before, forgetting my organic chemistry textbook. I seriously thought I would fail the course after that and even thought about dropping the course when the drop date approached. With Dina's help as a babysitter, I forged on with my study partner, all hours of the night at the IHOP, getting through it with coffee and cigarettes. Yes, I unfortunately still smoked the wretched cigarettes. I ended up making the B in the course and my study partner, earned the coveted A. Girl power, score two points for the female gender.

There's my organic chemistry war story. The moral of it is, no matter how difficult the situation before you, you can overcome it if you set your mind to it. It would have been very easy to give up and drop the course. Instead, I pushed even harder, knowing that failure was a likely result, given the circumstances. I really wanted it. I desired nothing more than to impress my father and show him that he didn't make a mistake by backing me up and encouraging my change of major to pre-medicine.

Upon proving myself with the organic chemistry course and other biological courses, my parents decided to put my medical school applications in full force. My dad signed me up for a Kaplan preparatory course before I was to take the MCAT (Medical College Admissions Test). This was going to be the most challenging test that I would ever take. The Kaplan courses were in Dallas and I lived two hours away in Wichita Falls. I didn't have a babysitter for Whitney for those nights of the week that the courses were offered. I still talked to Whitney's father as a friend. I asked Whitney's dad to drive me to Dallas once a week. That way, he would be obligated to babysit Whitney while I attended the classes. Otherwise, I believe that he would have said no. I don't think he got over our divorce very easily and in my opinion, he took it out on his relationship with Whitney. I don't think that they truly built a strong bond even though I stayed in the city for that reason.

I think maybe I attended two of the Kaplan classes. They seemed to help, but I stopped going because the two-hour road trips turned into arguments, so it just wasn't worth the efforts. I set out to study for the exam on my own. My parents had wasted money on the program, but I was determined not to let them down. When I finally took the MCAT, I did well. I scored above average, but I know I could have done better if I had been prepared. This wasn't an IQ test but rather a science knowledge test. My exam was largely physics-based and I hadn't had my year of physics yet in my undergraduate education. However, an above average score would still mean I was a candidate to get into medical school. I was always hard on myself and got upset if the score wasn't the maximum. I just needed to realize that being at least in the 50th percentile was enough to get into medical school. I was well above that, so I needed to chill. If you are not happy with your MCAT score, you can always retest after you take a break and prepare for it the second time. I would highly suggest going to prep courses such as the Kaplan program to prepare for the exam – especially if you haven't completed your core classes. They have online programs today so travel is not necessary. Don't try to take the MCAT (or any other college entrance exam) without being prepared.

At that time, I just needed to get through my senior year and send off the applications for medical school. Today, there is a website (www.aamc.org) that handles most medical school applications. You submit it to the site and choose the schools you wish to apply for and the site handles your applications. The professors submit their letters of reference online, directly to this site for the students. This is much easier than the old way.

My dad feverishly compiled my application packages and wrote my letter of interest and career objective statement. He was an alumnus at LSU Medical School and wanted me to go to school there. This would have been ideal since I would have been closer to my parents in southern Louisiana. He attended LSU for medical school and then did an internship at the Mayo Clinic. He wanted me to follow his footsteps. My parents had planned to hire a nanny to take care of Whitney during my medical school classes and so I could study without becoming a zombie. Everything was in place and for once, my future looked bright. Who would have known that an 18 year old boy would come into my life and change the course?

Points to Ponder: Even if the challenges ahead of you seem impossible, there's typically an alternate way around them. You can conquer almost anything if you are determined. Life is full of detours and some of those detours end up being better routes anyway.

CHAPTER 15 - ALWAYS BELIEVE

My friend had a younger brother who was friends with Jason. Jason was 18 and I was 23 years old. My friend had joked on occasion with how cute Jason was and what it would be like to come home to someone that looked like that. It escalated to a dare.

"I dare you to kiss him," she said, probably living vicariously through me, as she was married at the time.

"You are on!"

It wasn't like me to pass up a dare and this was a dare I later realized that I would have done un-dared. Jason was a handsome young man!

We drove over to her brother's house for her to introduce me to Jason. Wow, she wasn't lying. He was such a cutie. He looked just like a young Elvis. Not that I was a fan of Elvis, as he was a little before my time, but I could appreciate the resemblance. Jason and I immediately became attracted to one another. I had dated a few guys during my three-year stint of single-hood, but nothing serious, as I was dedicated to school. In addition, it was a little difficult to deal with a young daughter who was my number one priority. Not many young guys wanted to be tangled up with a single mom and Whitney definitely did not want me dating. Take heed to that, young girls! If you end up being a single mother, it becomes difficult to date and find men that don't mind playing daddy while you get to know them. I don't blame them, either. I am sad to say that I couldn't date a man with kids. It's too much baggage and headache – especially if the kid doesn't want you there. However, that's just me. I know there are plenty of people who feel differently.

After being at Jason's house a couple of times, he decided to cut to the chase. He chased me around the house for a few minutes before cornering me and laying a big kiss on me. I won the dare that had turned into a five-dollar bet.

From that moment on, Jason and I spent every second together that I wasn't in dance or at school. He and Whitney got along great and we became a dynamic trio. Eventually, I got Jason a job at the dance studio as the office manager. This worked out great. With my new focus on Jason, there was less focus on getting into medical school and my undergraduate education. The semester I met him, I ended up dropping down to one course from five courses. I was unable to concentrate on studies with this newfound love. This was a huge mistake. You should never let anybody interfere with your plans for your future. I could have stayed on course, on track to LSU, with a nanny for Whitney, with Jason still in my life. Instead, I allowed my hormones and my clouded brain to change my motivation.

After only six months of dating and eventually living together, Jason surprised me with a birthday marriage proposal. I said yes to marriage and eventually no to medical school. We traveled south of New Orleans to visit my parents for spring break. We were playing billiards in the playroom and I have no idea how it came about, but an umbrella in the playroom closet became the focus of the conversation. It was signed by none other than Mr. Ben Hogan, the legendary golfer. My mother explained whom the umbrella was signed by, and Jason was more than impressed. I casually mentioned he was some older dude that gave me golf lessons at my old country club one time. Jason proceeded to explain to me that it was analogous to Whitney getting a golf lesson from Tiger Woods. That's when it sunk in how awesome it was to have been trained, however in a limited capacity, by someone that was an icon.

While visiting, I had to break the news to my parents that I was going to need another two semesters of school. I explained that I was behind because I had dropped some courses. I had to let them know that I would not be going to medical school in the fall. They were more than furious. I was set for my third, in-person interview with LSU and had to cancel it. Then, I topped the news with a cherry by telling them I was engaged, and had set the wedding date for the following fall. My parents were more than outraged and disappointed that I had decided to change course from medical school and marry a teenage dance studio office manager. I didn't mean to hurt them, I was in love. Blinded by love. In my opinion, if you are truly in love, love will follow your course. There was no need for me to change my trajectory over this new relationship. If it were meant to be, Jason would have followed me to medical school. Hindsight is always wiser.

I asked my friend Dina, Shalah's mother, to be my matron of honor. Whitney was my junior maid of honor and the dance studio owner and another friend at the time were my bridesmaids. We had two gay best friends at the dance studio that stood by Jason along with his brother who was the best man and my brother was a groomsman. It all worked out great except my parents only gave me $1500.00 as a wedding budget. I don't think they believed the marriage would last or maybe they were still angered that I was making the decision not to go to medical school? I don't know and don't wish to analyze it, but it was my one shot at a real wedding. This was a wedding that I decided to participate in, and I was going to make the best of it. Not to ruin the story, but as of this date, we have been married eighteen wonderful years. Boy, were some people wrong about us!

Not long before this time, I had opened my first business (Nandi's Dancewear) by sub-leasing a space in the dance studio and selling dancewear. Because of the business, I had a tax ID and figured out how to get around the Dallas markets to purchase things wholesale. I made the wedding budget work and my wedding was quaint but memorable. I held it at a historical bed and breakfast and the afternoon wedding was awesome with a nice reception afterward with all of the wedding traditions taking place. It was very memorable and I stayed under budget.

A month or so later, after the wedding bliss had barely worn off, I found out that I was pregnant. I had seven months of school left. The baby's due date and my expected graduation date matched.

Points to Ponder: Never allow a new relationship to throw your path off course. You will certainly regret your decision later. You can have a new relationship and remain on track with your dreams. Find a way to make the new relationship fit into your life like a puzzle piece without distorting anything. It is challenging but possible.

CHAPTER 16 - BACK IN BLACK

I was pregnant and married again, but the second time, to a nineteen year old. Wait a minute! Stop the press and shut the front door! I was pregnant and married to a 19-year-old the first time! Well, but this time, my pregnancy interfered with my education. Wait! Stop the press again! The marriage interfered with my education the first time as well! Was this a curse? Why did my life seem like the movie *Ground Hog's Day?* Let's take a big sigh here and bathe in the irony. At least the second marriage to a nineteen year old, I was in love and happy.

Jason and I lived in a three-bedroom apartment for about $450.00 per month. The apartment was decent, much better than I had lived in before. Due to my success in school, my parents had previously bought me a convertible and we had two pet ferrets named Fred and Samantha that my brother had given us as a wedding present.

I only had the spring semester to get through being pregnant. I was going to finish my degree and then figure out what to do with the Bachelor of Science in Pre-

Medicine degree later. I registered for my last semester with some of my hardest courses. I had saved them for last thinking that I could make a final push at the end with the light at the end of the tunnel called a graduation. I will never forget the course that burdened me this semester like no other. Histology. Histology (the study of bodily tissues) burns in my mind like a cigarette being extinguished on a mold of half-dried gelatin. I do forget the professor's name who taught the course, but I'll never forget her wicked appearance. She looked like an evil cartoon character. She had short black hair with pin curls framing her white wrinkled face, lips sketched in with red lipstick that invaded the surrounding crevices. She always carried a long cigarette holder with a smoldering cigarette. In 1995, people were allowed to smoke in the hallways of the buildings. I know, disgusting. Moreover, it was so dangerous considering it was a science hall with flammable chemicals inside of the laboratories.

She explained on the first day of class that there would be only two examinations. A mid-term and a final exam. That was it. The exam would consist of her announcing various microscopic structures (i.e. Haversian canal, areolar connective tissue, elastic cartilage, etc.). We were then required to choose a slide out of our slide box, and using a light microscope, we were to find the structure that she announced on the slide that we chose. When we believed the microscope pointer was on the right structure, we were to raise our hand and she would view our microscope's pointer and check our score sheet right or wrong. On the first day, we were assigned a study partner and one key. The key fit into the lab bench that held our slide box that contained over 100 slides of various things like a section of a tongue, a scalp, body tissues, etc. We were given a schedule of the open lab times when we were allowed to come into the lab to study our slides with the microscopes. This was before the internet. Yes, life existed before the internet. The best that you could do for supplemental materials was to go to the library and look up things in medical textbooks. I chose to study in the lab with the slides. If my test was going to be a hand's on test, it was best to study with a hand's on approach.

The midterm was approaching and it was time for my partner and me to study. I attempted to call her for a few days and I finally got a hold of her. This was also pre-cell phones and it was much harder to get a hold of one another. She couldn't meet up to study until the night before the exam but promised we'd stay in there as long as we could before being kicked out of there. She couldn't meet me in the lab until 5 PM. I begrudgingly accepted because she had the key to the lab bench to get to our slide box.

The time came and I anxiously waited in the lab with anxiety coursing through my veins. Nightfall came and my partner with the lab bench key never showed. I panicked, raced home, and studied the diagrams that I had written out on paper during class. These diagrams were going to look nothing like the actual slides, but they were all that I had. There was no book to the course. Because I waited until the night before, there was nowhere that I could see the pictures of the slides. I was in big trouble. Not only would Whitney and Jason be at home and demand a portion of my attention, but also I had inadequate materials to study. Why did I wait until the night before? I had always been a quick study, and knew that I could cram the night before. After all, I was seven months pregnant at this time and didn't feel comfortable sitting on a hard lab stool. The test was comprised of microscopic pictures, not words or concepts.

The day of the midterm, I visited the professor during her office hours to explain what had happened. She told me that my lab partner had dropped the course the day before and that I could have went to the office to pick up the keys to the lab drawer to get my slides. However, I didn't *know* that she had dropped the course and I wasn't scheduled to meet her in the lab until 5 PM, after the biology office closed. The professor had no sympathy for me and stated that it was nearly time for the exam. Realize, I was a graduating senior with no prior history of slacking. My reputation was great with all of the other biology professors. Nonetheless, I shouldn't have procrastinated and tried to study the night before. That was my fault and I owned it. However, I had crammed so many times before and maintained a highly respectable GPA.

The mid-term exam was a nightmare. I ended up making a 20%. I think that toward the end of the exam, she was marking things wrong because she expected them to be wrong. Who was I to argue? I was doomed. Here was the dreaded scenario: I was seven months pregnant, finishing a five-year pre-medicine Bachelor of Science degree. I had given up on going to medical school, and my husband Jason, upon my father's request for him to support our growing family, had enlisted in the United States Air Force. Jason was due to move us all to California in June immediately upon my graduation from college in May. There was only one other exam to take in this course and that was the final. I had to do something or I wasn't going to graduate. I would have gone five years of school, against all odds of being a teen pregnancy drop out, for *nothing*. Just to reach the finish line and collapse before the ribbon hit my chest.

I begrudgingly made another appointment with this professor to talk about my grade. She already knew what happened to me regarding the mid-term exam and my partner in the class. She was unwilling to do anything to allow me to make it up. She proceeded to tell me to drop the course because there was no way that I would pass. She said that she had never in her life given a 100% on an exam to a student. She said that with me being nine months pregnant at the time of the final exam, there would be no way for me to focus to be the first to make a perfect score on one of her exams. The impossible 100 on the final exam and the 20 on the midterm exam would average to a final score of 60, which was barely a D. However, this would be passing and I could graduate and move to California with my family as a woman with a college degree. I didn't have a choice; I had to shoot for the perfect score if I wanted that college degree – the degree that was against all odds for me to have in the first place as a pregnant high school dropout.

I decided to study alone for this impossible feat. I got my own key to the lab bench and made it a point to stay after class and practice on the slides every day. At least I studied whenever I could, given Whitney's weekly dance and gymnastics schedule. I also continued to teach at the dance studio until I was almost nine months pregnant. I had to do this so we could afford for Whitney to continue in her dance and gym classes. I knew deep in my heart that if I didn't give it my all to pass the histology course, I'd never go back to school. If I transferred to a school in California, I'd need at least thirty hours to graduate at the new school and that simply wasn't going to happen, especially not with a husband, seven year old, and a new baby.

The day of the final exam, I went into the lab, looking like I was carrying a huge pumpkin in my belly, but with confidence. I knew the material very well. I didn't have a question that I could earn the first 100% that this inflexible professor had ever given.

The exam was more than challenging, but I did it. I won the battle against her. There was no way that she could even argue it. During the exam, I saw her straining with me on a few questions, but I was ready to run down the hall for back up with the chair of the department. I knew I was right on each question and she wasn't going to stop me from graduating, even though I could see it in her eyes that it burned her to give me the perfect score. She didn't even smile, she didn't even praise me, she seemed angry when she wrote the score on my exam, as if I had just defeated her in battle.

I forgot to mention that the final exam was a comprehensive exam. This means that I knew the complete material from the entire course, including the mid-term material of which I scored a 20%. Armed with these stats, I made one last appointment with the professor to discuss the possibility of bumping my grade from a GPA-murdering D to a C since by earning a 100% on a comprehensive final; I showed that had I learned the material better than anybody in the class did. I knew it better than any student in the history of her courses did, for that matter. She abruptly responded with a no.

I took this to heart and realized that I could take her cold, callous nature and learn how to be a great professor one day by actually caring about my students and doing what is right. First, I think she was out of line by only having only two major grades to assess her students. My opinion is that three graded opportunities should be the minimum and four to five is optimal truly to assess a student's progress. As a professor, I always have a failsafe of a makeup exam or an end of the semester cumulative exam because we are all human and make mistakes. You are allowed one mess up during the semester, but if it continues and you mess up a second time, then you deserve what you get. However, one mistake should never be the determining factor for your grade. It's just how I see things and this histology course is the underlying reason. Things happen for a purpose, I suppose.

Here's a side note: I am very flexible as a college professor when it comes to grades, but I am definitely not a pushover. Given my experiences with this course, I can honestly say that given the same situation, I would have given the student a C in the course. A grade of a C is not a competitive grade to say the least and a student in this exact example would have clearly learned the material to an A standard. However, due to the midterm mistake, a two-grade penalty would have been sufficient.

However, that would not hold true for a course with more opportunities for grades, curved exams, or a course where a grade is completely dropped. I've had many students come into my office at the end of the semester and demand an A in the course when they've clearly earned an 87 or 88. In my classes, the final scores typically are inflated by curves on individual exams, a dropped or replaced exam grade, and extra credit calculated into the final score. In the case as described, the student would earn what they deserve which would be a solid B. An A is a competitive grade, and a student should definitely never be awarded an A unless they earned it, period. Realize that having an A when you didn't actually earn it is not fair to your competition when you are both applying for programs. That's my take on it and how I conduct my evaluation of students.

It was the day of my college graduation and I was back in black. This time, it wasn't a black maternity wedding dress but rather a graduation gown, which actually doubled as a maternity dress. I looked hideous being only 5'1 tall and nine months pregnant. I had never walked a stage before and was determined that I would see what it felt like. It was exhilarating. I couldn't wait to do it again on another day. Completion of anything is addictive. It gives you a natural high and that's what you should strive for in life. Completing, achieving, mastering and conquering.

Points to Ponder: Always assume that you will not be given any handouts or second chances. Even though most people are reasonable and forgiving in this world, never expect anybody to give you anything or be flexible. You should always depend upon yourself to earn everything. Then, when people do things unexpectedly, you appreciate them so much more.

CHAPTER 17 - KARMA SUCKS

I was a colonel's daughter. I had previously received many of the same benefits that my dad enjoyed on the military base. People had treated me as royalty everywhere I went when they heard about who I was when I was a teen daughter of a high ranked official. On the military bases, it was like I was famous. I loved it!

My new husband Jason was the lowest level airman on the base. As a military wife of a lower enlisted soldier, I no longer received the double salute when I drove my car through the base gates. I received the irritated sideswipe hand gesture with a snarl. Nobody cared who I was anymore. I traded my colonel's daughter ID for an airman's dependent ID. I had to remove the colonel sticker from my car and put the lackluster airman sticker in its place. It was karma and she was back to slap me in the face. Remember when I said that as a sixteen year old, I drove through the gates repeatedly so the military police at the gate would be required to double salute my car? Well, this was a harsh payback and I deserved every snarling sideswipe gesture that I received as I drove through the base gates.

I had been seeing the physicians at the military hospital and was treated differently from when my dad was the colonel in the hospital. They didn't remember who I was, as the personnel changes frequently on military bases. Even if I told them my dad was a colonel, it didn't matter; my main sponsor was my husband, the low-ranked airman. The hospital visits were like a cattle call. I was greeted by a no-personality medic doing the minimum they could do with the least amount of comforting conversation as possible. The experience was impersonal and had I not already endured a pregnancy before, I would have felt scared.

The conversations of the baby's delivery day began. They informed me that I would have to deliver the baby without anesthesia. They stated that they didn't want to do anything that would put the baby at risk. They said that administering anesthesia of any kind, such as an epidural that I successfully had during my previous delivery, was a risk. What? That was insane! I still question this line of thinking. I think stressing me out with that much pain was a bigger risk to both the baby and me than giving me an epidural. I suppose that the reason why I didn't get anesthesia is that I wasn't a high enough ranking military dependent to get the added costly procedure. This is my theory, at least. We tried to bargain with a civilian anesthesiologist to perform the procedure. We agreed to pay the difference. The military base hospital said no. We asked if we could have a stipend to have the baby off base. They said no. I was to either pay full civilian price on an airman's budget for the delivery or deliver my child on the military base free of charge. Great. I was in for a nightmare. I know that many women elect to deliver their baby's natural without anesthesia. I'm not one of those women.

I was over a week past my due date and had to be induced with Pitocin, which is a hormone drip that causes labor to commence. I made it through the horrible pain of natural childbirth with Jason right by my side. The pain of natural childbirth was unbearable, rendered me speechless, and Jason said every pore in my skin opened up at once and sweat poured strangely from my body. I remember getting to the point where the pain was so intense; I couldn't register any further pain in my mind. I reached a point where I knew the pain was getting worse, but I could not put a further intensity on the perception of the pain. It was not only hard to perceive, but it's also difficult to describe. I am not telling you this to scare you if you haven't already had children. My advice is if you are considering natural childbirth, be mentally prepared for a painful adventure. Take classes and get into the correct mental state. I've done it both ways (i.e., with anesthesia and natural), so I can honestly say if I had to do it again, I'd chose the epidural route.

Finally, the moment arrived when my handsome and talented Zakk was born. We had already done a sonogram that told us his gender, so it was no surprise that he was a boy. Family and friends waiting on the other side of the door burst into the room to gaze at him and enjoy his first cries. It was a highly emotional experience and most of all; Whitney was there to see her beautiful baby brother for the first time. Zakk was handsome at 7.1 pounds, and his birth was just as lovely of an experience as having Whitney – with some added pain. Upon his birth, my mother took my loving ferrets away (Fred and Samantha), took the keys to my convertible, and gave me a minivan. It was embarrassing for such a young mother to be driving a minivan, but it was a free car so what could I say? Nothing.

Points to Ponder: Live by Karma. If you do something wrong in life, it will come back to get you. You can't run from it, so embrace it. Live positively and it will bring you strength.

CHAPTER 18 - IT WASN'T ENOUGH

My family relocated to California per my husband's orders from the military base. Jason became stationed at Edward's Air Force Base, working on F-16 jet electrical systems. The pay wasn't great, but the base benefits made it bearable. We lived above our means in a brand new four-bedroom home off the base in Rosamond, California. The rent was $900.00 and definitely was out of our budget range. My parents had supplemented our income our entire marriage up to this point. My parents wanted the kids to live in a good environment, but wanted us to get on our feet. I appreciated my parent's help - beyond what words can express. However, just so you know, in case you are not fortunate enough to have parents providing you with cash - it wasn't necessary. We could have made it on our own. We just wouldn't have lived in as nice of apartments or homes as we had at this point, but we could have made it. My parent's supplement afforded us to live above our means for the benefit of our kids and that's honestly not a good life lesson. I think you should earn your way 100% - especially after you are married and raising a family.

I had my BS degree and had owned my own retail shop previously, so I landed a job as a manager of a shoe store in an outlet mall. Wow, this wasn't exactly medical school. I stood on my feet for hours each day, selling men's shoes in a boring retail strip, thinking about what my life could have been at this point had I taken the other turn towards medical school.

I didn't regret Jason, I didn't regret Zakk, and I still didn't regret Whitney. However, I regretted being in California. I regretted not going to medical school. It didn't have to be this way. I was experiencing a *reality check* for the year that I lived in California. It was stressful living under my potential, thinking this was *it*, not knowing where I'd go with a career. My brother and his wife moved to California and it helped to pass the time and made me forget about my career inadequacies. Not that there is anything wrong with being a retail manager. It just wasn't for me. I didn't see myself on the path of managing a shopping complex. It wasn't my forte or my interest and definitely had nothing to do with my five years of higher education.

I decided that my issues with authority and past life on a military base as a dependent princess was just too much for me to handle. Jason and I decided that I would move back to Wichita Falls and go back to MSU for graduate school (to work on my Master of Science) so that Whitney could be by her other side of the family. This ended up being a huge mistake once again. Why did I care that Whitney lived near these people? I don't know. As I always say, hindsight is always clear. The right decision would have been to go to LSU and be by my parents for once. However, I felt compelled to give Whitney a chance to know her biological father. This was a futile effort, in my opinion. I moved to Wichita Falls and moved in with my best friend Dina (my matron of honor) and her family. Whitney was more than thrilled to be able to live with Shalah, her best friend. Jason had some military things to tend to for a few months and he would catch up with me in Wichita Falls once he officially got out of the military.

It was the morning of the GRE (Graduate Record Exam) which is the exam you are required to take to get into graduate school. I was feverish, so I grabbed a thermometer and it read over 104F. Crap! I felt miserable but this was the last exam date before school started and I needed this test for admission into graduate school. I ambled to the test site, Tylenol and bottled water in hand, and started taking the test. I didn't think I could finish it. I progressively felt worse with each hour. I stumbled up to the proctor to try to turn it in - unfinished. Through the cloudy haze of my illness, I was giving up. The proctor gave me a pep talk and convinced me that I could muster enough strength to finish. She ran and got me some cold water, a wet rag, and another Tylenol and I proceeded to finish the exam. To my shock, I actually did well. Again, I scored a six out of six on the writing section and the other scores were good. I was admitted and registered for my first classes and picked my major professor who I had taken for zoology as an undergraduate. He was a great teacher and had a super lab program in mammalogy (the study of mammals). I was interested in microbiology, so we mixed our interests, and I studied the intestinal tract flora (residents) of ground squirrels.

The only problems I faced at this time, as a single mother of two, was having to support my kids and go to school. Yes, I say single mother because Jason was still in California, having to pay for our house and its associated bills with his small military salary. He still had to tie up loose ends with the military, so in the meantime; I was in Wichita Falls by myself. I didn't have family to support my two children and me. One cynically positive thing was that I had slipped back into my anorexic ways after I stopped breast-feeding Zakk, so at least I was cheap to feed. Let me reiterate, I would never suggest nor condone anybody having an eating disorder. It is a very serious disease and you should be treated immediately if you feel that you are suffering from one.

Points to Ponder: Live your life with minimal regret. You only have one shot to accomplish everything that you can.

CHAPTER 19 - AGAINST THE ODDS

A Bachelor of Science in pre-medicine was nearly useless as a degree unless I went to medical or graduate school. It was great for the jobs that simply required having a degree, such as my shoe store manager position, but it was a broken path and not one in which I could live.

Living with another family was great in some ways because I wasn't alone and I enjoyed their company. However, not so great in other ways because the dad of the other family would go on weird rants when his wife wasn't around about how smart you had to be to dig holes. I did love being with my friend Dina and Whitney loved being with Shalah, her little sister Amber, and her adorable little brother Scottie. The kids had a blast living together.

For the second time in my life, I essentially found myself with very little clothes. I think I might have left a lot of them in California by mistake, but I certainly didn't have the cash to restock my wardrobe. I needed a job and at this point, I had a BS degree but couldn't work a nine-to-five job because of graduate school. Most of the courses offered were during the day and my lab was active during the day. I had never done biological research before and needed as much training as possible.

I applied for various retail positions in the town. I finally landed a spot at Dillard's in the women's fragrance department. I am a huge fan of perfume and had heard that we were given the old testers when the new ones came in, so I was more than thrilled to accept the job. I was hired at $8.75 per hour. I thought this was awesome given that the last hourly position I had held was only $5.00 per hour. Whitney and I reunited with our dance studio, but my studio salary was very miniscule since I had a lot of trade-offs going on with Whitney's dance, gymnastics and my competition squad.

I had a BS degree in pre-medicine making $8.75 per hour. Something doesn't sound right about that, huh? Good thing they issued me smocks to wear as a uniform. That solved my wardrobe issues. Moreover, for school, it definitely didn't matter what I wore to class. I think I mostly wore my Victoria's Secret flannel PJs or my dance practice attire. Who cares? By then, I was definitely not a fashion snob anymore.

The only problem about this new set up was Zakk. He was one year old and I didn't have a daycare that I trusted. Dina was very busy with her new job at the prison and with her family. Without family in town, I had to find a baby sitter and one that could watch Zakk in the evening so I could work at Dillard's. I had a daycare for the daytime, however. The daytime daycare was one that I learned to trust as I had sent Whitney in as a spy and she reported that all was well. Whitney was easy; she did whatever Shalah and Amber did, so I didn't have to send her to a babysitter at night. I finally found one daycare that was an around the clock center. Again, this was in the very early days of the internet, so there was no way to look up reviews on the place.

I dropped off Zakk in a playpen under the care of the teacher for the night. When I picked him up after my four hour shift, he was in the same position, reddened eyes and an uncontrollable rhythmic gasp as if he had been crying for a long time. The teacher was in the rocking chair with a newborn, ignoring Zakk as he cried in the playpen. I can only assume that he cried the entire time I had left him and they had done nothing. After getting him home, it took a while for Zakk's rhythmic gasps to cease. I was sickened. Dina was sickened. I had Dillard's reduce my hours and I worked it out with Dina where Zakk didn't have to go to a daycare at night. You just never know whom the people are in which you are entrusting your children's well being without a solid referral. Recommendations are essential to select the right daycare for your child. In present time, you can easily do a Google search on any daycare to view the history so the research is now easy to do and you can make a more informed decision.

My first semester of graduate school for my Master's program started and I was doing awesome. My fellow students were great. If only these folks had been at Nightmare High, my life would have been so much better. Please believe me, once you get out of high school and into college, you will see that it is like night and day. Even if you hated every day of high school, your college years are going to be fun. Get ready for them! The atmosphere is so much more compassionate and there's a kindred spirit in the air – unlike cliquish high school. Then, when you get into graduate school, the camaraderie between graduate students is even stronger.

My major professor knew I had a fear of snakes and believed that you can't be a biologist and be afraid of animals, so he placed a large king snake named Oreo onto my desk in the lab a few times. As he left the lab, he warned me not to hurt Oreo as I put him back into his aquarium. I got over my fear of snakes quickly, but I admit that I often rescued the snake's lunch mouse from the aquarium. I'm sure that Oreo the snake didn't like me very much because he often grew hungry after I performed the *Operation Mouse Rescue*. Sorry snake lovers and PETA officials, I prefer mammals. I was a mouse advocate, not a snake hater. Oreo was probably glaring at me daily through his aquarium, chanting snake voodoo curses at me as his tummy growled. I never let him go without a mouse on consecutive feedings, so stop freaking out. Oh well, I survived and so did the snake.

Whitney had a growing interest in science and spent a lot of time with me at the university. She ended up being a valuable assistant at times. I took a field biology class and we were required to trap rodents in the field. Whitney really loved oatmeal and my fellow graduate students and I soon recruited her to chew up oatmeal for our rat traps on our field expeditions. Whitney held the oatmeal container, chewed up a pinch of oats and spit it out onto our hands for us to use on the traps. Such a mother-daughter bonding experience, huh? Whitney had a blast on our trips and ended up getting valuable field biology experience by the time she was eight years old.

Knowing that Whitney loved science, I helped to arrange a fourth grade field trip with her teacher from school to tour our newly renovated science hall at the university. My fellow graduate students and I arranged a tour of the science hall that included the biology department, chemistry department, geology department and ended with a cool planetarium show. During the biology portion of the science hall tour, the kids were able to look at all of the live animals, the dissected animals, the bones, microscopes, and other cool experiments we had prepared for them. My part was to hold Oreo and allow the kids to pet his body and feel the scales. I held Oreo behind his head with my right hand closer to my shoulder, above and away from the kids for safety. He wasn't a mean snake, but you never know with wild animals. He ended up biting me a few times and even pooped on me. I think the kids made him nervous because he had never done that before. When I received the thank you letters from the fourth grade kids, I was shocked to find that of the entire science hall tour, their favorite part was when I was bit by and pooped on by Oreo. Kids crack me up!

It was 1996 when my love for teaching was born. The first course I taught was a botany laboratory course. The newbies were always stuck teaching botany even with no interest in plants. It was a rite of passage, I suppose. The first day, I introduced myself as I took a seat in a chair in the front of the laboratory. To my surprise, the chair whizzed out from underneath me and I fell straight on the floor. Of course, you won't be shocked to know that the class laughed. Do you blame them? It *was* funny. This ignited my future style of teaching, however. I liked it when they laughed, even though my back hurt from slamming on the dirty lab floor. I didn't want a boring class, but it shouldn't have been at my expense. Currently, I don't undergo fake falls on the first day, but I do maintain a lively classroom and inject humor, no matter how poorly executed the humor is, during my lectures. I am still teaching today, but I never know when I will put away my laser pointer and expo markers for good.

When Jason finally joined me in Wichita Falls, nearly three months after I left California, it was a blessing. I had missed him more than I ever knew that I could and it was sad since he had missed Zakk's first steps and his first birthday, which were coincidentally on the same day! We bought our first personal computer and my interest in writing commenced. My father was writing a murder mystery novel at the time, intermingled with poetry that he was publishing and we corresponded on the phone. He taught me how to write fiction. He is more than a brilliant man. He is a Mayo Clinic-trained surgeon, poet, novelist, philanthropist, and Minor League Baseball player. I think that is where I get my over-ambition from, actually.

Jason and I soon moved into our own space, a nice three-bedroom apartment. Well, I say nice, but I should say as far as apartments in Wichita Falls go, it was nice. It was also really close to the college as well as the mall. Jason got a job at Dillard's with me but in the electronics department. We arranged our schedules so we could take care of the kids and it all worked out fine. I always felt sorry for the single women in my fragrance department and wouldn't fight for sales so my salary soon dropped to $7.00 per hour since I didn't make my sales quotas. All I have to say about that is – it sucked.

I was on the two-year plan to finish my Master's degree, which is typically at least a three-year degree. It had been done before, but my major professor said it would be difficult and was rare to finish a Master of Science degree in that amount of time. I worked on my research any open time that I could muster between teaching at the college, going to classes, studying and working at Dillard's. Don't forget, I was a wife and mother of two children as well. However, when you want something and have ironed out your goal, you have to stick to it no matter what happens. If you fail to achieve one goal in your life, it is all too easy to fail in others. If you never fail, and won't *allow* yourself to fail, you will be compelled to reach each goal you set for yourself. It's all right to extend the time to achieve your goals, but do not give up on goals.

I graduated with my Master of Science degree at the end of two years with honors. It was May of 1998 and I put on the gown with a hood and sash with the additional honor cord. As I walked the stage for the second time in my life, it was a spine-tingling experience to know that I had earned yet another diploma to hang on the wall. Knowing inside that I hadn't even graduated high school gave me a heightened sense of accomplishment.

Points to Ponder: You can accomplish nearly anything that you set your mind to do. Even when things look impossible, never give up. In most situations, you will eventually achieve your goals.

CHAPTER 20 - OCCUPATION, ANYONE?

It was finally time to leave the armpit for the last time. I couldn't go further in school at MSU and I didn't see much need any longer for Whitney to be in the same town as her biological dad since in my opinion, he was not maximizing his time with her. The job market was also difficult and we yearned for a city with a broader entertainment selection for restaurants, concerts, and other venues.

We set our attention on the DFW area. I grew up in Westover Hills, which is on the Fort Worth side of the metroplex. We didn't know much about the rest of the metroplex, but knew we wanted to stay on the Dallas side of things, as there were more jobs available. Both Jason and I applied for jobs and even I applied around the country to major federal agencies. I had an MS degree; I should have been able to command big dollars, right? Well, I believe I applied for about 250 jobs including the CDC in Atlanta, the FBI, among other types of jobs in Dallas such as a medical technician, lab technician, and at school districts for secondary teaching positions. Why not apply to schools? I had taught college level courses for two years so why couldn't I teach high school students? I immediately landed an adjunct teaching position or two at some colleges that I would continue to hold during all of my other years of employment. To date, I have seventeen years of teaching experience and have won an award for excellence. In the early days, the adjunct teaching positions were a good supplemental income for my family. They later became a hobby that I continued to do, even when I didn't need the money. I have an unsurpassed love for teaching to this day. I feel as though my students are all my children and I love to watch them grow, learn and succeed in life.

I received letter after letter in the mail of how I wasn't qualified for various full time jobs. Frustrating! How could I have seven years of education and not be qualified for a decent job? It was because I didn't have experience. However, how can I get experience if I'm in school? It is so frustrating. My advice to you is if you can possibly get a job within your intended field while you are in school, do it. Even if it is an unpaid internship – it's better than no experience when you get out into the work force and compete for jobs.

Finally, Jason landed a sales job selling commercial alarm systems. The vice president of the company believed in him since he was ex-military so they hit it off immediately. Soon after, Denton Independent School District hired me as a secondary teacher. I was to make $27,000.00 per year. I had a Master of Science degree in Biology, two years of college level teaching experience, and seven years of higher education behind me and I was to earn 27K. It was frustrating, but I had to do what I could to help support my family.

We found a home in Denton. It was three bedroom and brand new. At this time, we were not prepared to purchase our own home since we didn't know the metroplex and were not sure Denton was where we wanted to stay. Both of the kids were young enough to stay for a year or two and then we would settle in for Whitney to finish school. I had learned from my own experiences that you don't relocate a kid past middle school. You let them stay in their hometown, with their friends, and allow them to graduate with their class. It had just become my rule given my own experiences.

Right after the school year began, I received a packet in the mail. It was from Quantico in Virginia, where the FBI headquarters are located. They wanted to interview me for a forensic position in their crime laboratory. I would have to train as an agent even though it was a crime laboratory position. The training was sixteen weeks of which I would not be allowed to see my family. I wanted to do this so badly, but I had already signed a year lease in Denton and signed a contract to teach a year of school for Denton ISD. Furthermore, Jason was quickly rising to be a superstar in his company. However, the strongest reason that I declined on the FBI interview was that I couldn't imagine having to leave my children for four months.

Jason soon became the number one sales representative at his company in the nation and his income was going right along with the title. We researched DFW for a new home and found that Lewisville ISD had one of the highest school ratings in the metroplex. We looked at the homebuilders in the area and found one that we were pleased with and soon built our first home. Getting the home loan was stressful, as we had limited credit. However, we did it without a co-signer and we were more than proud of ourselves. We had simply opened small credit accounts and purchased a couple of cars and were timely on the payments. You'll never believe this, but we had to pay an erroneous four-dollar library fine before we were granted the loan. Seriously? A library in California claimed they didn't get their book back on time, but I distinctly remember dropping it off before I left for Texas. In addition, they admitted the book was returned and the due date was after I moved to Texas. Do the math! It is more than obvious that I didn't take a flight to California to turn the book in late. Whatever! I paid it just to get my home loan. Lesson learned – life's not always fair.

We moved into our brand new home, a four-bedroom one-story home, in Lewisville, Texas, which is a northern suburb of Dallas. This is where we lived from 1999-2004. We eventually built a very nice swimming pool in our over-sized backyard. Things were looking up for us and our future careers looked bright. We purchased our first luxury car, a Lexus IS-300, and our children had absolutely everything that they desired. We were so proud of ourselves that we had finally made it as a family, on our own merit, living on our own income without my family's monetary assistance.

To our despair, a large corporation named Tyco unexpectedly bought Jason's smaller alarm company, Smith Alarms. With any big corporate buy out, the little people are always tossed to the side. In addition to the takeover, the CEO at the time was indicted for fraud and went to jail. I believe he still might be there, actually. Jason had won sales representative of the year for the second year in a row and we were due another free vacation – the year prior, we were sent to the Ritz Carlton in Cancun, Mexico. Upon the Tyco buyout, they removed this rewards program, conveniently after Jason had been awarded the honor. I think that Tyco still owes us a Puerto Rican vacation at the Ritz Carlton. I'm just saying.

My secondary school teaching job had ended as I was only on contract for one year under what they called an emergency certification. I still maintained my college adjunct teaching position, but that didn't pay but maybe $500.00 per month during the semester. At my high school teaching job, I had received a performance review by the principal and it was excellent. I earned nearly all five out of five points on the evaluation directives. When we discussed signing a contract for the following year, I was told that I would have to become certified or at least begin working on a secondary certification. This meant that even though I had a Master of Science degree in biology, I would have to go back to school and take 26 hours of college courses in education. What? Didn't the principal just hand me a review that was almost flawless – meaning, my teaching skills were nearly perfect? Does this make sense in a logical world that if I had a Master of Science degree, had taught three years of college, and had been evaluated by the principal of the school as being nearly a perfect teacher – then, why would I be expected to go back to college to learn how to teach? I wasn't going to spend more time and money in school to learn how to teach for a job that paid 27K per year. Forget that! I hit the want ads in the newspaper and the school district lost a good teacher.

Within a very short time, Jason's salary dropped to zero. Tyco management altered his sales territory to a smaller area, changed his pay plan to 100% commission, and took his established accounts away. Tyco had their own sales representatives for their alarm company (ADT) and they didn't want the Smith Alarm sales representatives competing with their established sales representatives. This was disguised as a merger, but it honestly didn't work out that way. Instead of laying Jason off and paying him a severance, they made it impossible for him to make a living. I think this type of corporate strategy to get rid of employees without having to pay them is evil. This crushed us financially. I finally landed a job as a chemist, but I didn't make enough at my new job with a salary of $30,000 to support our family. We had always lived above our means and budgeted to the dime with our expenses. We were never prepared for a financial disaster such as this. Let's call this the Great Bon & J Financial Collapse #1.

The bill collectors started pummeling us with phone calls and there was nothing we could do to hold our head above the water. Our family, house, and cars were all that mattered at this time. This was the year 2000. It was our first credit crash. Both of our credit ratings dropped and we were ruined financially.

At one point, our electricity was turned off, they charged us a huge deposit to have it turned back on, and of course, we didn't have enough money. My brother had found recent success in the mortgage business and was able to wire me the money to bail us out to get our electricity back on. Most people don't have a wealthy relative to get themselves out of financial distress. Had my brother not been there for us, I most likely could have called the electric company and worked something out.

This happens more than you know and to the very best of people. Never be ashamed if it happens to you, it's not always your fault. Yes, we should have had a savings account for a rainy day. However, when you live paycheck to paycheck, it's too difficult to do that. Hindsight is clear; we were not ready to live in a 155K home with a 35K pool in the back and own two cars worth 32K and 36K. We should have stayed in an apartment for a few more years until our income rose. Nevertheless, you can't be your own parents all the time and you will make poor decisions in life. We are all human.

Hating my corporate job as a chemist catapulted me into taking my writing career more seriously. I had already written my first novel, *Mentan*, which is an unpublished work to this day. It's about an underground society living off the powers of the Earth such as fire, water, electricity and ice. Every birth is a quadruplet and each is gifted with one of these powers. The story takes you on a journey to the surface of the Earth equipped with villains, betrayals and romance. Maybe one day I'll revisit this, but back in 2000, I could wallpaper a wall with rejection letters. I know that my writing skills were not developed at this point. I was too new and was taking the hard route in learning how to write fiction. My genius father had co-written many chapters of *Mentan* and showed me how to develop characters and plot lines and even write dialogue. Many of the agents and publishing houses that bothered to write back gave me great criticism and direction with how to fine-tune my art of writing. To this day, I thank them for taking the time to reject me.

Most people would give up with that many rejection letters. I can admit that I thought about giving up a time or two. Being rejected is a tough thing to take. You have to grow thick skin and realize, you haven't lost, and you just need to get better.

I heard a time or two that you should never publish your first novel so I revisited my second novel that I had started while working on my Master of Science degree - *Take Heed to your Nightmares.*

Points to Ponder: Rejection and failures in life should motivate you to do better, not discourage you.

CHAPTER 21 - CORPORATE LIVING

I continue to work diligently on my second novel, a horror suspense thriller, during the time that I worked as a technical service chemist at a chemical corporation. I worked the nine to five and wrote at night with every available minute that I could get free. I despised the corporate environment more than I can express in words. My intense loathing for the atmosphere of company backstabbing is sprinkled throughout the book.

Back to my issues with authority, I didn't like having a boss. Especially a boss with fewer diplomas on the wall, telling me what to do when I knew what was best. Nobody else in my department had above a Bachelor of Science degree. I had earned a Master of Science degree and it seemed that it didn't matter to a soul, and I was treated the same as the rest of the employees. I was somewhat delusional by thinking I would graduate with a Master of Science degree and all of a sudden be respected by peers. What truly matters in the corporate world is experience. The degrees on the wall only come into consideration when promotions come into play. Sometimes, not having a degree will cause you to not be promotable (or even hirable) – even with years of experience. It's always best to get a Bachelor's degree (at a minimum) prior to starting your career. If you don't know what you want to do as a career, chose a general studies major. At least you have a degree. My husband Jason has been in a situation where not having a degree caused problems – even after being ranked #1 in the nation at what he did (stay tuned for this story).

My boss at the chemical factory eventually got into trouble for sexual harassment of many of the young girls at the company. Never put up with sexual harassment of any kind in the workplace. There are federal laws (Title 7) against it and human resources should take any claims very seriously. There are also retaliation laws to protect you for reporting it. My boss was removed from his position in our department. I spotted him one day in a cubicle they had made for him over in the laboratory building (instead of corporate headquarters) that was boxed in with three walls with the opening to the back wall of the room. He was not allowed to contact anybody in the company and was given paperwork to do all day. All of our paperwork from our department was sent to him and he that is what he did each day. Why would they not fire this man? I am clueless. However, they left our department with only have half of a job so it gave us time to play, I suppose. Some things that go on with corporations do not make any sense!

There were issues of backstabbing from my coworkers when it came to assigned projects from the lab. For example, the lab director gave me a project to start working on to develop a mosquito larva pesticide for ponds and other stagnant bodies of water. I had barely got started on the research when during a lab meeting; a male coworker in my department submitted his research proposal for the project I had very recently been assigned in a lab meeting. I thought you only saw this crap in movies or on snarky television series. It really happens? It wasn't that I was slacking, I was only being thorough and taking my time to do it right. I'm certain his proposal was unfounded and lifeless, but the fact that he undercut me on time earned him the project.

I realized that I was simply too nice of a person. I wasn't really cut out for this cutthroat rat race. I decided to start looking for another position, but back in academia where I had spent seven happy years of my life by this time. I definitely wasn't afraid of hard work. By this point, I finished all tasks given to me in record time and with excellence. I always received outstanding reviews with any job I had - besides at Dillard's when I didn't make my sales quota. I figured it wouldn't be as *corporate* if I worked at a university.

I finally landed a job at a university for $45,000.00 per year. This was a 15K increase and even though the hours would be a little longer, this would help us get out of our financial crisis. My husband had since moved to another alarm system company and was making a decent living again, but as sales goes, it takes time to build your accounts and start making real money. I still taught my adjunct teaching positions during the nights and weekends and both of my kid's had after school activities that caused my husband and me to be booked out to the max.

My new job title was research compliance officer. This meant that I would be hovering over all research at the university to make sure it was being performed within federal, state and local regulations. Due to the nature of the job, I quickly made a few enemies with the professors who made statements to me such as:

"You are not a doctor, so what do you know about research?"

I was baffled! Professional people such as professors talked to administrative staff like that? What? This was degrading and more than annoying. I had a Master of Science degree, had performed research, written my thesis, and even published it in a peer-reviewed journal. I worked with one professor who only had a Master's and she was actually nice to me and always took my advice with compliance issues. This lady earned her PhD during the time that I was employed there. Once she earned the title, she morphed into one of the snobby, entitled professors that argued with me over compliance regulations. People, please never let a title or authority go to your head and change who you are! Working with these faculty members irritated me so much, the thought of getting my PhD just to shut them up coursed through my brain. My boss and I eventually moved over to a sister university, but most of the faculty members were not any better over there when it came to research compliance. It must be a syndrome or something?

On occasion, I noticed that some people were allowed to work from home in our department. When I asked if I could work from home for a few days, such as the time I broke my foot playing tennis, I was told no. Therefore, I had to drive 45 minutes across the metroplex with a broken right foot and yes, I am right footed. My job was largely reviewing research protocols, sending emails, and writing memos. All of this could have easily been done from home, but I wasn't allowed. This didn't make a lick of sense. I was a hard worker, received excellent performance reviews, yet I wasn't allowed any flexibility. Maybe because my desk was a catchall for projects? I don't know the details of why others got to work from home on occasion and it's not worth speculating. The hard cold fact was when I asked during a much-needed time, I was told no. This made me despise my job even more.

After a few years of working hard and dealing with a bunch of BS, I more than hated the environment in this department. I don't like it when your work doesn't speak for you, but in my opinion, it seemed as though how much you kissed up to the boss is what earned you glory. Again, my issue with authority reared its ugly head once again and I soon applied for other positions in the university.

Our financial situation was getting better each year even though we were immediately unable to catch up with many of our unsecured credit accounts and they were calling us at all hours of the night. One debt collector had a neighbor come over and tell us that somebody was trying to get a hold of us and that it was an emergency. I never knew that a creditor would go to such great lengths to embarrass you like that. We were doing all that we could do to pay off our debts and stay afloat with monthly bills, but it was just taking time. Creditors continued to harass us, as well as our family members, daily and we were telling them the same thing that we told them the day before – we will pay when we can. That was never good enough.

In addition to the debt collector madness, we were victims of identity theft two times during this period that added to the financial chaos. I remember the bank calling and asking me how my credit card was swiped in Las Vegas and Dallas simultaneously. They nearly acted as if it was my fault! How is that for customer service? The Las Vegas con artist had not only wiped out my bank account but also opened all sorts of credit accounts in my name as well. The fact that our bank account was wiped out for a few days, caused checks to bounce for my bills that I was paying at that time. This led to late payment fees on the bills that weren't paid on time, insufficient funds fees from the bank, and absolute chaos. That was one of the most frustrating issues I've ever dealt with in my life. This crook even ordered pizza to his home and signed my name incorrectly on the receipt! I can only assume that the bank had the police catch this thief, but we were not in the loop. We ended up having to change banks because our accounts were in such shambles. We ended up paying out of pocket for a portion of this identity theft simply to end the confusion and get our accounts in line. I'm certain that banks have a much more streamlined way of preventing and dealing with identity theft than they did a decade ago.

I eventually landed a promotion and departmental transfer at the university as the Director of Institutional Compliance, making about $64,000.00 per year. Research compliance was only a portion of what my expertise would be with this new position so I had to engage in a swift learning curve. In my new department, I worked with Karshena, now my very dear friend, as my only employee. She is such a genuine person and I love her and her lovely family. Eventually, I hired a good friend as a favor and we became a team of three.

I was never a demanding boss. I was easy going and we worked as a team. I have a problem with authority, so why would I ever act as what I despised? Put it this way, I believe that Karshena still would like me to be her boss to this day – enough said.

For the life of me, I can't decipher why, in only a period of a couple of months, my good friend thought that she deserved a raise or promotion. She drove me crazy by begging me to ask my boss for a raise for her. I was the director, barely made more than her, and I was the one with experience and a graduate degree. However, *she* needed a raise so soon? It didn't make any sense. Every time she spoke about it, she pushed me further away, making me hate my job more every day. I began to realize that she was not really a friend. I can't stand people who use others for personal gain. As a friend, I had hooked her up, but in a very short time, it just wasn't enough for her. If anybody had deserved a raise, it was Karshena for being the veteran in the department, but since we all had received recent raises with our promotions, we were not due until the start of the new academic year. Without title-changing promotions, that's how academic raise schedules work.

I had to get out of there and start working on my PhD. Thanks to my brother, my husband had received a job opportunity in the mortgage industry as a subprime mortgage banker making well over six figures.

Within a month of Jason working at the mortgage company, a friend of ours put enormous pressure on Jason to get him a job at this new company. Jason told him that it would be impossible while he was still in training, but maybe he could hook him up in a few months. For the record, it is very difficult for a new employee to make a recommendation for another person, especially a person with no experience or a college degree, to be hired. As a new employee, you are trying to impress others and assert yourself in your job, not play recruiter for your friends. It's rude to demand that a friend get you a job, anyway. Call it coincidence, but when this friend didn't get a job at Jason's company, we didn't hear from him or his wife for long period.

We were eventually able to afford for me to quit my job and I did so without regret. Here is some sage advice - don't mix business with pleasure, and tell your friends to get lost when it comes to working together. Stick to it!

In the meantime, my loathing for office environments catapulted me to finish my novel, *Take Heed to your*

Nightmares. It was time to get the new edition of the Writer's Market and find some publishers to send me some more rejection letters to paper my walls with, but I was ready for them.

Points to Ponder: Your business where you earn money should never mix with your personal life, unless you are self-employed. Then, use great scrutiny when mixing the two or you are likely to lose friends and your sanity.

CHAPTER 22 - THE FATED THREE LETTERS

Jason's success in the mortgage industry was what ultimately catapulted us to where we are today. He was able to support the family in a lifestyle that we had only been able to see on television while I focused on my PhD and writing career. We took limousines nearly everywhere we went, drank Cristal champagne at over $500.00 per bottle, dined at the finest restaurants, sat in the VIP suite wherever we went and took elaborate vacations. We even treated friends and family to expensive dinners and vacations. My son was in elementary and middle school during this time and had every electronic device available, wore Prada wind suits, custom athletic shoes, and every athletic jersey that was available. My daughter had a store's worth of designer clothes and everything she asked for. We certainly didn't respect money but had enough that we were able to accrue a six-figure savings account in record time. As you will see, there is a lesson to be learned from this experience. If you don't respect money, it will not respect you – stay tuned.

I had dabbled with murder mystery parties in the early part of the decade, but I revisited them during this time. I was again, on a tight plan of completion of my graduate studies, which was three years. My new major professor at The University of North Texas (UNT) stated that three years was nearly impossible to obtain a PhD (starting at an MS level) but could be done if I worked every given moment of every day. It is a minimum of six years if you start straight after your Bachelor's degree, by the way. Therefore, that is what I set out to accomplish. I still kept my adjunct teaching position, as I loved teaching. This is when I realized and proved to myself that teaching was in my blood. I couldn't go a semester without teaching a class or I would have felt lost. I love my students and am proud of them when they do well and frustrated with them when they fail. I certainly didn't need the money at this point and could have used the time for other things, but I felt a duty to the students to be there for them. The end of the semester emails from the students who appreciate my love for teaching is what has always kept me in the teaching game.

I had always been known for giving extravagant parties for Whitney. During her younger years, I always tried to out-do what I had done the year before, coming up with new ways to do fun, memorable things on a small budget. As the budget grew, so did the parties. I worked my way up to hosting elaborate casino parties and murder mystery parties in my new North Dallas home, which is what we referred to as the Scarface Mansion.

Let's take a moment to discuss the Scarface Mansion. Jason and I purchased brand new luxury cars - a convertible Mercedes Benz and a Hummer - while we still lived in Lewisville. Our neighbors rushed over upon seeing them in the driveway, asking if we had won the lottery. We were searching to upgrade our home at the time and were looking at various properties with our realtor on the weekends. One day, Whitney and Jason did a search while I was at school and found a large stucco Mediterranean home with a heated pool and spa, a huge marble-floored foyer below a catwalk, multiple gigantic crystal chandeliers, a mirror-backed wet bar, switch-on fireplaces, etc. This was a house of luxury. It was beautiful and it was ours in record time. I didn't even see the home that Jason purchased prior to moving in – he and Whitney said 'trust us.' This became our home for the next four years.

Thinking of the huge hurdle that this pending PhD was as it loomed in front of me, I sat still for a moment and sifted through stress-ridden thoughts. I closed my eyes and entered a near meditative state. I convinced myself that it was three years in the future. I saw myself graduating. I ventured into a month past graduation, grabbing the feelings of finishing my MS degree, my BS degree and how it all seemed like a blip on the radar screen of life. I knew that no matter how hard that I would have to work or how difficult or complex the material would be that I would have to master, I could do it and *would* do it. I would complete it. If you will things to happen, they will happen.

You might think at this point, well, I'm going to put this book down now since she had a husband that was making so much money she could quit her job. You may think that you cannot do that, so you are out of luck. You are probably not in my situation at that time. Most people are working a full time job and barely making ends meet. Unfortunately, a growing number of Americans are not even making ends meet. Yes, my husband was doing well at the time and afforded me the luxury to quit my job. However, we also didn't have to live the way we did in the Scarface Mansion, and I could have taken advantage of many scholarships, loans, and grants to fund my way through school. Learning from my mother who wouldn't take a paying job on the military base in Germany, I didn't want to apply for any of these things and take from others that needed it.

Let's discuss what is available to you. Change your line of thinking now. Most PhD programs have variable sorts of funding for their candidates. You often have all of your tuition paid for by scholarships or by your major professor's grant, as well as some of your living expenses. You would be surprised at the deals that the government or even departments are offering for graduate students. You can actually earn a decent living, have your school paid for, and get your degree all at the same time. Most people are very unaware that this exists and think that you'll have no income and be out tons of money for tuition and books. Take your time, search around for programs that you are interested in, and ask the professors what type of funding they offer for their graduate students. You may be amazed at what you find, and don't get discouraged if some of them act as if you are crazy for wanting them to pay you to attend their program because many do not have funded programs. Believe me, there are graduate schools that will pay you to attend by giving you scholarships, fellowships, stipends off their grants for research and other programs such as teaching assistantships. There was a person I knew of with a $25,000 per year fellowship in addition to tuition and books paid for each semester. Remember when I said I made $27,500 per year as a secondary teacher with a Master's degree? Well, yea, you can go to graduate school full time and nearly make the same as a career position. Look into it! Don't delay!

We rented our Lewisville home out to a family for about a year before deciding to sell the property. The renters eventually stopped paying us, and left a foul taste in our mouths about being property owners. In addition, we eventually had to *pay* the buyers a grand total of $25,000 when we sold our home because we had foundation issues with both the home and pool and had to have them repaired. Our tenants never reported any of these issues to us, so the year that they resided in our home and the problems worsened. This cost us more money for the repairs and an ultimate loss of property value. My advice is, don't build, renovate. Perform thorough research on homebuilders and pool builders before you hire them. Building a home and a pool was the biggest hassle I have endured in my life. If you have to be a landlord for whatever reason, screen your tenants thoroughly, and stay in decent contact with them while they are living in your property.

I worked on my PhD research at least twelve hours per day, even driving on the ice and snow to Denton from Dallas to do research protocols during the holiday seasons. Don't judge, in Texas we don't know how to drive on ice very well at all! It was so difficult to stay focused while everybody was having fun around me. I remember taking part of my research home and tending to experiments that I had set up in my laundry room during a huge New Year's Eve bash that I hosted at the Scarface Mansion.

My doctoral classes were more than difficult, and my dissertation was a gargantuan amount of work. Not only was designing, performing and analyzing my research extremely time consuming, but I believe my professor and I had revised my dissertation manuscript over fifteen times by the time I was ready for the committee to review it. I had to pass two major hurdles before graduation – the doctoral exams and the dissertation defense. Doctoral exams are designed to test everything you should know about your field as a PhD. They test you on the basics to the most complex topics and are open to anything in the field. With a PhD, you are the expert; there is nobody you can turn to for the answer, so failure of even one question is not acceptable. If you fail, I believe you might have one more shot to pass (depending upon your committee) or you could be kicked out of the program. The exams have two segments – an oral test and a written test given by each of the five members of the doctoral committee. The exams were an utter nightmare, but a rite of passage. After sweating every ounce of sweat in my body for a two-week examination period, I passed all exams with excellence.

Then, it was time for my dissertation defense. Again, I had to face my committee and defend my research. The public was invited to attend this event to watch me turn into a bundle of nerves at the podium. I had always been a great public speaker, loved to be the center of attention, but the dissertation defense was my kryptonite. One of my committee members was from Canada and had flown to Texas for my defense. He was the most experienced in the field, and I figured he would be relentless – especially to make his trip worthwhile. I knew that if I failed the dissertation defense, there was a chance that I would be asked to start over on a different research project and / or that I wouldn't be awarded a PhD, even after all of the effort that I had put forth. They don't hand out PhDs in science by any means, so if somebody has one, please realize they earned it!

At my defense, I was to present my research and then it was open to the public for questions, followed by my committee's questions, problems and concerns. This was the first time that I was nearly unable to speak in front of a crowd. It was almost unbearable and somehow, I forged through the presentation and my internal autopilot took over during the arduous questioning. When all was done after about three hours of a relentless interrogation, my committee kicked everybody out of the room and deliberated on whether to award me a PhD. I think I was in the hallway for over an hour, waiting in angst. They finally allowed me back into the room and my committee members gave me a hug. I was awarded a PhD and it was time for the champagne party back at the lab.

Looking back, the three years whizzed by and as I had predicted, the hard work of my PhD seemed as though I had climbed a daunting mountain and I was now rolling down the other side, laughing and enjoying myself. It was the most difficult three years of my life, frustrating and nearly impossible at times, but I had finally earned my terminal degree in my chosen field - developmental physiology. I was a doctor and would forever hold the title. The day I graduated, it was an out of body experience. I had finally reached my goal. It took me ten total years of hard work and dedication, and I graduated with honors, with a 4.0 GPA. This earned me spots on the Cambridge Society Who's Who list, Phi Kappa Phi Honorary Society, National Scholar's Society, among other organizations that honored academics that had achieved their goals.

I took a stretch limousine with all of my friends and family to my graduation, drinking Cristal champagne on the way. We arrived late, and I barely made it in line to walk out to my seat for the ceremony. At the graduation reception, I put on a tiara that said *Princess Grad* and didn't take it off until I got to Las Vegas – where we continued the graduation party. On the way to Las Vegas, our family was in the front row of the first class section of the airplane. A dog barked behind me and so I looked between the seats and noticed a little dog in a purse.

I said playfully, "Awww, how cute! What's its name?"

A blonde girl with the dog in her purse grimaced and responded bluntly, "Ace."

The woman sitting in the seat next to the girl glared at me as if to warn me to turn around.

I turned around to Whitney and told her how rude they were and just as I finished whispering to Whitney, the dog barked again. Whitney turned around and looked through the seats and not only recognized who it was with the dog, but also noticed the ticket on the drop down table in front of her friend. It was Carrie Underwood, the American Idol winner. I was incensed that she would be so unfriendly to me when it was her dog barking on the plane! Maybe I should have considered that she was having a bad day and she didn't want to deal with fans? Lesson learned – if you are a celebrity, you should never act rude to anybody in public, as people tend not to forget about it and might include it in their autobiography.

Points to Ponder: You can't get anywhere without hard work. Sometimes in life, you have to make sacrifices in order to get ahead. The fact that huge parties were held at my house while I was studying for my PhD should show you that there are times when you just need to focus on what needs to be done in order to accomplish your goals. You can always play later.

CHAPTER 23 - FINANCIAL TITANIC

My academic achievement was met with bittersweet misery the day the mortgage industry collapsed. This was The Great Bon & J Financial Collapse #2.

Jason worked for a mortgage bank and had risen to what was termed the *President's Club* with the enormous amount of loans he was processing each month. He was a superstar in his company, which was no surprise, given his work history. He eventually was able to hire a friend named Chip (separate from the one that was begging for a job before) onto his lending team and in record time, Chip was enjoying a great salary of $10,000 per month. See, if the original friend from Chapter 21 had been patient, this would have been his job. However, this ultimately became the second time we were burned by hiring an ungrateful friend (remember the friend that I hired at UTA that compelled me to quit my position).

Let's focus on Chip. Chip's wife told me that her husband previously made $4000.00 per month at his clothing sales job. He was hired by my husband with no mortgage experience and soon after, he was bringing home

$10,000 per month. I've tried not to use all caps, but this time, it's necessary to get my point across – HE SHOULD HAVE SHUT HIS MOUTH AND BEEN GRATEFUL. You might wonder how I knew Chip wasn't grateful. Well, I had to hear about how ungrateful he was from his wife, who I thought was my friend. However, this is what she said to me within a little over a month of Chip working for my husband's team: "When will Chip get to earn real money and stop working for everybody else?"

She didn't say this after years of Chip working for my husband but rather only after a few months. What the heck? I really don't know what gets into people's heads with all of this greed. Does greed cloud good senses of weak people?

Now I'm going to explain what happened to Jason's lucrative job in easy to understand fictional terms. You are a neurosurgeon. You are making a large profit in your field and you are revered as one of the most highly respected neurosurgeons in the field. You are supporting your family; you have dreams and plans for the future that include your hard work and high salary. Now, without warning…every human's brain disappears. There are no more brains on Earth. You are out of a job. What do you do?

Jason was making neurosurgeon money and within a period of six months, subprime lending was no more. His job had vanished, along with the economy. The US entered the recession and we were in trouble again financially. At this time, I had graduated with my PhD, and had finished my second novel. I had written many murder mystery parties over the last decade and we decided that I would open my own murder mystery company online. I didn't have any experience with an internet business, but I would immediately start learning the field. I bought books on SEO (search engine optimization) and internet marketing as well as web design and html. If you thought I worked hard on my PhD, learning all of this stuff was ridiculous. We had maintained a standard of living that I didn't want to see vanish and this time, we had much farther to fall. I didn't want to go back to an apartment and the primary reason was the kids. We had worked excessively hard to get to where we were that day. I didn't want the kids to have to give up anything. I could easily give up the champagne, trips, parties and limos, of course. Looking back on it, they were such silly things to waste money on, nonetheless.

After my husband's company closed its doors due to the mortgage crisis, Chip tried to weasel his way back into the failing subprime mortgage business by gathering all of my husband's old accounts from the company. My husband had already warned him that the subprime mortgage industry was done, and he should look for another job. Chip, with no history of experience in the mortgage industry, believed his limited experience had afforded him the knowledge of a seasoned veteran and that he knew better than Jason and all of the experts in the field. A mutual friend told me that Chip's wife said the following: "Don't tell Bonnie, but Chip took all of Jason's accounts and is planning on taking them over when the mortgage industry comes back. He will finally be able to make his own money one day soon."

All I have to say is that it has been over five years now, so I hope he found a way to support the family while he plans this hostile takeover. Hey, be sure to turn out the lights when you finally leave the subprime mortgage industry, your betrayal will never surface, but your soul turned an ugly shade of black. Lesson learned again, don't mix business with pleasure. Those closest to you *sometimes* seem to be the ones who least have your back when it comes to the workplace.

Parties (more subdued, less extravagant) were hosted at my house and I became a slave to my keyboard. Literally, my friends would come over to swim and have fun in my backyard and I stayed in my office, working. This was necessary, I was the future. Jason didn't have a degree and Jason's job had vanished. He tried to apply for many bread-winning positions, but since every person in subprime lending was also looking for a job in the financial industry, it was impossible for Jason to land an interview. You might wonder – if Jason was at the top of the subprime lending industry - why wouldn't he be snatched up by an employer in a related field? I spoke earlier about when not having a degree became a thorn in Jason's side. Even though he had been a superstar in the subprime mortgage industry, without a degree, he couldn't land an interview with jobs at a fraction of the salary that he was used to earning. There were simply too many unemployed competitors flooding the market, and companies were able to increase their qualifications for employment. Most companies changed their policies to require a degree. It was quite demoralizing for Jason, but things like that tend to make you stronger.

A potential literary agent instructed me to purchase and read *Strunk and White Elements of Style,* so I could make the necessary format and grammatical corrections before I submitted the manuscript for *Take Heed to your Nightmares* for publication. I took their advice, corrected the manuscript, and sent it out for another round of queries to publishing houses. At this point, I was near desperation to get a big break and bring my family out of imminent financial doom. I was the one with the PhD; it was my turn to be the breadwinner. I did finally receive a letter from a publishing company that was interested in my manuscript for *Take Heed to your Nightmares.*

During my scramble for lift off for my writing career, I dabbled in some random activities such as papermation and claymation to break apart the stress I was enduring. I was often called *Random Bon* and for a reason, I am random as hell. I came up with a cartoon series called Dr. D-Town, which is an animated short series about a drunken plastic surgeon who comes up with ludicrous ways of doing plastic surgery, but nobody thinks to question her methods. It is sort of my alter ego in a sense, but of course, the world can be glad I didn't go into plastic surgery with my cynical mind. I did have a glimmer of hope that maybe a comedy variety show would see it and pick it up for their show. I put everything I did on my YouTube channel and still do today. At a minimum, my friends used to get a kick out of seeing the random side of me. Unexpectedly, I had a silly idea to attempt a claymation. I never saw how they did such a thing, but I purchased clay, took subsequent pictures of shapes or people that I made out of it, loaded the pictures into movie software, and made movies of it. I know that I didn't create the wheel with animation here; it was done a thousand million times over and much better than I could dream of doing. I mean, Pixar cornered the market with animation and I knew I wasn't competing.

I did my first video of claymation and it was of a white clay man wearing sunglasses and a yellow clay man with a police hat on doing a choreographed dance to *Ice Ice Baby* by Vanilla Ice. I had been a dance teacher and knew how to choreograph a dance, even with clay men. A month later, I received a message through my YouTube channel by a research-marketing group that was representing the beverage conglomerate Mountain Dew. I thought it was a joke. They offered me $7500.00 to lease the animated video that they had discovered from my YouTube channel for a commercial for their new energy drink. They said they would give me time to think about it and if I wanted to negotiate terms, they would be glad to do so.

Here, you should hear brakes screeching in the recesses of your mind. Go ahead, allow it to happen.

They wanted me to negotiate for more money to rent one of my claymations that took me twenty minutes to make for a national campaign for seven months. Winning! I would have done it free just to say it was *my* clay dance video in the commercial. I accepted the offer with a huge Cheshire cat grin and laughed all the way to the bank. The funniest thing was being at a sports bar with televisions on the wall and seeing my commercial pop up on the screen. My brother was at a NHL hockey game in Los Angeles and saw the commercial on the jumbotron above the ice during half time. It was a surreal experience to see something that you created make its way to national television. To make it even more ridiculous, they approached me to continue the lease for another two months at another $2500.00 payment. I laughed again, all the way to the bank. Lesson learned, if you have the urge to do something random, do it! You never know when 10K will fall out of the sky into your lap. However, this money couldn't have come at a better time as our savings account was slowly being drained.

Points to Ponder: Never forget that no matter how fortunate you are in life, it can all disappear in a heartbeat. You should respect money and increase your lifestyle in very small increments as your income increases. Nothing is ever guaranteed in life and the most unexpected thing can happen at the most unexpected moment. As long as you realize that what you have can be gone tomorrow, you'll always be prepared for the worst and will rise above when necessary.

CHAPTER 24 - HOBBY TO LIVELIHOOD

I accepted a postdoctoral fellowship in a developmental laboratory at The University of North Texas (UNT). A postdoctoral fellowship is analogous to a medical doctor doing an internship and residency. Not like ten years of school wasn't enough, we need to train further before we can call ourselves real professors. I was also awarded an adjunct professor position at UNT. I still have this position, but will soon drop the reigns as I move on to the next segment of my life. However, I definitely did not earn enough money for us to live on as a family and our finances were sinking into the abyss, just as they had already done only seven years prior with the Tyco crash. It was a familiar, horrible feeling in the pits of our stomachs not to afford the finer things in life after working so hard to get where we were.

The Mountain Dew commercial ignited an insatiable urge for me to be on television. Being a famous actress was a dream that I had from the time I was only four years old. Remember when I said I didn't want to get off stage and that I fed off the crowd interacting with me? I always knew that one day, I would be a celebrity. I'm not there yet, but life isn't over until your heart stops beating.

In 2007, after graduating with my PhD, my friend from graduate school and I decided to apply for the reality competition show Big Brother. Why not? I could win $500,000 and get enough notoriety to sell my first book so it seemed like a win-win situation. It was the seventh season, and we were both big fans of the show. We spent time strategizing on our plans to win the season as we entered the semi-finals in the casting. But then, nothing. Neither one of us moved on to the next round, but I had met a new friend. A friend who would later change my life. Her name was also Bonnie and she was a reality television casting producer. I love her to this day and we shall always be friends.

She subsequently contacted me for future seasons of Big Brother, but the furthest I ever made it was the finals where they flew me out to Los Angeles to meet the executives before being cut and sent home. I decided that I didn't want to be considered for any further seasons of Big Brother. It was enough, I was done.

Bonnie did cast me for a reality game show. She convinced me that this would be a great opportunity, as it was only a one-day filming and I could win up to two million dollars. Wow, that would have saved my family's finances! I agreed to do the show, and my family members were secretly filmed behind my back. During the taping of the show, I was surprised to see their secret videos. It was a fun show, but it unfortunately never aired. Nonetheless, it wet my appetite for television. I loved the entire process, the cameras, the lights, and the attention. I wanted more, but my main goal was to be in movies. One day, I want to be on the big screen, even if I have to play an old wrinkly grandmother. I want to have a role in a feature film. In addition, you should know by now that I take my goals seriously, but this one doesn't have a time limit on it. As long as I get into movies by the time that I'm 70 – it's all good. Well, maybe 75 will be my goal on that one. Somebody has to play the grandmother, right?

Around this time, I had settled in on a publication deal for *Take Heed to your Nightmares*. The problem with the deal was that it was going to be eighteen months before my book would hit the shelves. This was not acceptable. I pulled it out of publication and started doing research on my own on how to self publish. Self-publishing is definitely not for everybody that aspires to become a writer as an occupation. It is nearly impossible to succeed unless you have a way to market your novels. A large percentage of people believe they can write a book and do so, everyday. With self-publishing, the marketplace is now flooded with books and you have to have an edge to rise to the top and be noticed. I was launching my business, which is an online murder mystery game store (MyMysteryParty.com). I thought that I could help market my novels through this retail business and with my other party hosting site called Party Host 411 (partyhost411.com).

I learned how to become an internet merchant, so it only made sense that I could figure out how to self publish my novels. I knew I would need to get some help from Jason, as he was the photographer and graphic artist of the family and was more software savvy than I would ever be. We created our publishing company, Zakkem Publishing. We are still learning all facets of the business as we publish my books and music and are about to launch it as an open for business company and accept other artists' work for consideration. This will be an exciting time for us in the future.

Points to Ponder: Life is about opportunities. You live once and why should you be concerned with failures or what people think about you? You'll never know if you fail until you try. Rejections and failures lead to success. Without them, you'll truly never know you have succeeded.

CHAPTER 25 - IN BUSINESS

After writing non-stop for many years, I finally opened the business My Mystery Party with only eight murder mystery party games. I had tested these games over time with my friends and family. I had hosted my own parties for over a decade and had worked out the kinks in the format. The thought of working this hard and falling flat on my face was frightening. I went live with the business, and then sat back and waited, expecting to fail, but hoping for the best.

It took about two weeks and I finally saw a red asterisk next to the word *orders*. I was unsure what it meant, but my heart started beating as soon as I realized it was my first sale. I clicked on the order link and saw my first customer. Everything had gone smoothly, the customer purchased with Visa and the download went as planned. My first happy customer was born.

Emails of interest started pouring into My Mystery Party's inbox and I happily became my own sales support representative. Why not? I was the initial webmaster, SEO manager, office manager, author, and more. The business took off and I finally saw a bright future for my family.

The only problem is that we had no idea what the ceiling of this business would be, but at least we were not capped out with my pitiful salary from the college.

Oh, wait. I forgot to tell you what I made at the lab as a postdoctoral researcher. I earned about $36,000 per year. I had risen to such a high salary because I had earned a PhD. Yes, I am being quite sarcastic. You should be shocked because when I would have been hired as a professor for my first position, I might have received a raise to $40,000 a year. May I reiterate, that is what I would have been paid with ten years of higher education and a two-year postdoctoral fellowship. Are you shocked? Appalled? You should be. It's ridiculous how little that professors are paid. Yes, with time and tenure, you can work up to a decent salary, so if you're a professor pulling in some bank, don't bother emailing me to let me know. We all know what you made when you were hired. Now I have heard that the biomedical engineering professors get a more decent salary to start out – but it's still going to be shockingly small compared to what they could make in the industry.

Our six-figure bank account was approaching zero. We needed about $50,000 in repairs to our home such as with sealing the stucco, replacing a marble shower, etc. We had little money coming in through my salary at the university; the sales were steady, but still not very high through My Mystery Party. Jason no longer had an income. Situations like this are great at revealing who your friends are. We had this one set of *friends* for over eight years. Over the eight years of friendship with this group, we had treated them to limousine nights, expensive dinners, you name it – we paid for it. We even took some of them on trips to Vegas and California – paying for all of their expenses. The dinner checks would arrive on the table and everybody turned to

Jason. As our bank account dwindled and the income wasn't pouring in, this became a scary time for a family of four with many expenses.

A large percent of Americans lost their home in 2008 when the mortgage industry crashed. It was ironic that the mortgage industry supported us getting to the top and then took it all away without notice. We got behind with a payment at the Scarface Mansion. We called the bank and they said that a government program had passed to help us out, but we were not far enough behind to qualify. Therefore, we got more behind with our mortgage payments. We called the bank again and tried to work out something since our income was rising with my writing enough for us to afford the payments, but the bank said there was nothing that could be done unless we caught up with all payments immediately. I have no idea what happened to that program, but it had evaporated in this short amount of time. This was a crazy time for the mortgage industry and policies changed from day to day as the government scrambled to fix the problems. This cold, callous attitude by our bank was shocking, given what was happening in our country.

We eventually found a very nice home to rent with a movie theater in it and the payment was ironically larger than our house payment at the Scarface Mansion. Looking at it from the outside, it does not make sense for a bank not to work with homeowners in a financial crisis, but rather to kick them out and make the property stay vacant for nearly a year. We had recovered financially to afford the payments; it didn't make sense that we still had to lose our home. Nonetheless, that is what happened. We had to move out, the bank took the house, and we watched it remain vacant for over year. The bank ended up selling it for 150K less than what it had appraised at when we purchased the home. Moreover, we could have simply stayed, made the original payment amount each month, and eventually caught up with past payments over time. No wonder our economy collapsed. Knee-jerk decisions by banks must have contributed to the disaster.

To make a ghastly story short, because the money ran out, so did the friendship with the group I spoke about previously. Jason and I were unable to be the same people that we were when we funded the parties and trips. They had no more use for us and that was that. Our friendship abruptly ended the day that I was accidentally copied on an email thread between two of the girls. They were making fun of us, saying that we were fabricating the money problems as an excuse not to want to go to dinner, etc. To this day, I'm not entirely sure if it was an accident that I was put on that email. Maybe they just had no use for us anymore since we were not as wealthy?

Here is a rule of thumb for selecting friends in the future. If you befriend somebody and they never once ask about how you are doing or how your family is (i.e. your children, etc.), they are not your true friend. If you invite them to your family member's birthday party (i.e. your child) and they say - *Why would I want to go to that?* Don't put them in your best friend circle on Google plus. Don't set out to make enemies, but keep these types of people at arms' distance and only give your trust to genuine friends that sincerely care about you and everything about you – as you would care about them.

Points to Ponder: I have always said that I live by karma. If you do right in this world, it will do right to you. Life takes care of itself, even when you think it has you down.

Another lesson here is that it takes risks in life to achieve the bigger payouts. If I hadn't spent most of my hours building MyMysteryParty.com or writing books with no guarantee of success, I would have never built the #1 murder mystery company or have published my novels.

CHAPTER 26 - CURRENT PROJECTS

Fast-forwarding in that hypothetical time machine I so desperately want invented, let's discuss the next few years briefly. Without the negative force fake friends in my life, it was time for Jason and me to focus on our goals. It was time to pump out mass quantities of quality games into My Mystery Party and help grow the business and take over the number one spot in the world. MyMysteryParty.com is still growing today, I am getting stronger as the C.E.O. with each experience, and I continue to drive my company into the right direction. If you ever decide to start a business, don't expect to be number one overnight. It takes years of hard work and dedication. You can't ever turn your back on it or your competition will take over. You wouldn't leave your purse on a bench in central park while you play flag football with friends, would you? No! Owning a business is the same scenario.

My husband amassed a full music-recording studio at our home over the years and we decided in 2010 to make a Halloween Dance Party Mix CD. We had always ended our house parties with recording a fun dance song with our friends, so we thought – why not publish a CD? I wrote the lyrics, Jason wrote the music and we came together as the musical group *Party of 2*. We are currently working on another Halloween and a Christmas CD that is scheduled to be released sometime in late 2012.

My start up publishing company is called Zakkem Publishing. Through the creation of Zakkem Publishing, Jason and I learned not only the self-publishing trade for books, but also music. My husband is a photographer, graphic artist and an accomplished musician. He is highly skilled at the art of mastering radio quality music. To our excitement, we learned how to navigate our way through publishing music media and were accepted on iTunes along with other musical download sites with our Halloween CD (Monstrous Halloween Dance Party Mix). Everything that you need to know about how to do things can be found on the internet. It just takes patience and tenacity. If you want to know how to make the best muffins in the world or how to make a robot – how to videos and sites dedicated to showing you how to do it are at your disposal.

As of this date, I have published my sixth book through my publishing company, Zakkem Publishing. By 2012, I have released four fiction titles (*Take Heed to your Nightmares, Chronicles of Zombie Town, 614 Scarlet Ct.* and *Fiona Frost: Murder at Foster Manor*). Scarlet Ct. and Zombie Town are actually coupled with murder mystery parties from My Mystery Party. It is always great to integrate your businesses if you have multiple directions. These two novels are simply continuations of the story lines of both murder mystery parties, but are both great stand alone stories – you don't have to do the mystery party and vice versa. The novels are great for giving to party guests as favors of the murder mystery party.

You might wonder why I chose to publish through my own publishing company and why would I not sign with an agent and /or a publishing house. As you know by now, I have an inherent aversion to authority. That's the first reason. I pulled out of a publishing deal for *Take Heed to your Nightmares* because I didn't want to wait eighteen months. I think that is ridiculous and I wanted full control of the release of my novels. At this point in my life, I don't see the need to hire an agent or a publishing company for my books. I have started my own company; have everything in place, and am about to start accepting submissions from other artists. I hope to make plenty of artists' dreams come true in the future. It has been a long haul for both Jason and I to gather the knowledge that we have on all aspects of the publishing world. We are a collective team and hope to one day grow our publishing company to be one of the premiere online publishing companies in the world. This is another one of my many goals.

I am about to launch my tutoring video series on my YouTube channel (BonBlossman) – Dr. Bon's Science Theater. I plan to start with biochemistry tutorial videos and work my way down to middle school science videos. I've purchased three puppets that I will make into characters for my videos – each having a various expertise in science. I find that adding humor is the best way for students to learn difficult concepts. It isn't for everybody, of course, but I've found with my feedback in all of my years of teaching, that my sense of humor is appreciated.

My daughter Whitney completed esthetician school in Florida, but the Texas requirements are more intense. She plans to attend esthetician school this summer and will start planning to open her own med-spa in the future. She is also pursuing movie roles and trying to get into acting as well. Fingers crossed that she can make a break!

Currently, my daughter and I are engaged in a campaign to prevent bullying. We are very passionate about anti-bullying, especially with the LGBT (lesbian, gay, bisexual, transgender) community, as they are the typical targets. Childhood cruelty is one of the worst social issues that we are facing today. The suicide rate is high among LGBT bullied teens and this type of tragedy that is becoming an epidemic is preventable. If we get to the parents and teachers, promote awareness, and educate students about the ramifications of their actions, we can at least make a dent in this repulsive behavior. I fully support the Trevor Project, which promotes awareness for teen suicide and hosts a valuable teen suicide hotline, GLAAD, which promotes equality for all, and GLSEN, which is an organization that is infiltrating school systems and promoting awareness to put a stop to bullying. My daughter and I plan to continue in our campaign.

My husband is starting his own online music company and plans to open soon - just as I did with MyMysteryParty.com. His internet music company will be the place to go for downloadable music to be used in projects such as rap songs, commercials, school assignments and more. He will also offer music mastering and mash ups.

My son is a duel athlete with a rigorous schedule. He is on two soccer teams and plays varsity football as the kicker. He is nationally ranked as a kicker and we hope that he can acquire a college scholarship in the near future. He is also an aspiring electronic music producer (Official Zorrex) and he is currently working on his first CD of electronic dubstep music and on his DJ career at the young age of sixteen. He will work along with Jason and Zakkem Publishing to release his first CD.

Points to Ponder: The sky is the limit as long as you are willing to work hard to get there.

CHAPTER 27 - THE REALITY OF TELEVISION

I had swiftly worked my way through my writing career into the top percent of this nation's earners and I supported my family in style. We were comfortable, happy, and were enjoying each other as well as life in general.

Unexpectedly, I received a phone call from my friend Bonnie, the casting producer from Los Angeles. She had a proposal for me. It was about a show focused on mothers and daughters in Texas. The show was to be called Big Rich Texas and would air on the Style Network.

The first thought about being on this new show that featured mother and daughter duos was that Whitney and I would not be like the other mothers and daughters. We had always been more like sisters and I never truly fit in with my peers (mothers of daughters Whitney's age). Whitney and I talked about it and Whitney was on board and wanted to move forward. I was a tad more apprehensive and did my research on the show. Whitney was in school at the time and was a pre-medicine major. She was proving herself in a community college and then had plans to transfer to a four-year university. She was doing well and I was proud of her progress. She had previously enrolled in college two times prior, once when she was seventeen, and both times, she had dropped out. I was afraid that filming this television show would knock her off track and for the most part, I was correct. We are trying to get her back on track now, but it appears as though the pathway has changed direction. Maybe this is for the best?

No news here – we ended up signing on to do the show. Having cameras around was stressful, but you learn to live with it and it simply becomes part of your day. The first day Whit and I had cameras around, we both wanted to throw up out of nervousness. That feeling went away very quickly and towards the end of filming, it started to feel weird without them around. We were just being ourselves and if we were not likeable to the fans of the show, we knew that we would have nobody to blame but ourselves for who we are.

I can honestly say that in season one of Big Rich Texas, I was uneasy about the way I was portrayed as a whole. It's as if I was a seven layer chocolate cake, and all anybody got to taste was the icing. I just felt as though everything that is *me* wasn't a focus, but only my silly side was the hub of my portrayal. My daughter and I appeared as day-drinking, plastic surgery-acquiring airheads – but whatever gets an audience, right? I can honestly say that I didn't expect to be slanted that way on the show. I am definitely known for being random and silly, but in my normal life, I do not drink alcohol during the day unless it is a special occasion and my plastic surgery endeavors was limited to boob repair after kids and some Botox and fillers for anti-aging.

It wasn't even mentioned (other than in my press release cast bio) on the entire first season that I am a writer by occupation. This was the primary reason why I wanted to do the show – to get more publicity for my novels. However, my fans, whom I love so dearly, are sometimes admittedly shocked to find out that I wrote one book, much less multiple. It shows how editing and the choice of footage can twist your persona to the public. In the end, what you saw on the episodes was definitely my personality but only a skim off the surface of what I do, what I am, and who I am as a parent.

Whitney and I are as close as a mother-daughter duo can be. We consider ourselves as best friends - even though we both have our own set of individual friends. We've come to the realization that if you truly want somebody to have your back and always do right by you (and vice versa), the mother and daughter relationship is one of the true, unbreakable bonds that you can ever have the pleasure of sharing in life. It is not that you can't have as strong of a bond with a friend, but from my experiences, it is rare. Whit and I cherish what we have in each other, not taking one day for granted. When I am criticized for being a bad parent (of an adult child) because of our relationship, I take it in stride – some of that is necessary for television ratings. If we were shown as being perfect, how entertaining would that be, actually?

I realize that my parenting duties are over for Whitney and they ended the day that the rebel turned eighteen years old. The only way to stay in her life as I am is to be her friend and offer guidance, as she will accept it. Those quick to judge others, I have found, are lacking somewhere in their lives, so they search for fault in others. When I tried to over-parent the adult Whitney, she moved out of my house and then away to Florida with friends. Therefore, I have a choice to have her in my life and be her friend, or try to parent her and have her live across the country. I'll take her as a friend. At least as a friend, I can attempt to have some input in her decisions and get her on the right pathway. No matter what, Whitney will do whatever she wants to do and I am now helpless as a parent. Take that for what it's worth and ask yourself what you would do. She is probably one of the most kindhearted people but stubborn as heck when it comes to decision making. I love her more than words can express no matter what.

Looking to the future, it seems filled with goals and aspirations higher than I've climbed before. I just hope there is enough daylight. I hope that I have inspired you to follow your dreams and achieve your goals. There is no reason on this Earth why you should have an idea to accomplish something and not get it done. It might take you a long time, but never get discouraged. Never allow another human being to force you off track from your ambitions and you should always live for you.

Final Points to Ponder: In the end, you come into this world alone and leave it the same way. You are your best friend, so start living for you. There is no better time to start than today.

BON'S LINKS

My Mystery Party at MyMysteryParty.com is the preeminent internationally acclaimed murder mystery party company and a #1 choice for party hosts. We provide unique murder mystery party games that encourage exciting interaction through multiple rounds of game play. Super easy host instructions and hosts play along with their guests! Download and host a party today! Party Host 411 at partyhost411.com is your one stop shop for all of your party hosting needs. If you are looking for a theme, etiquette, games, costumes, or other party ideas, look no further! Dr. Bon wrote The Official Party Host Handbook and you shouldn't host a party without it! Visit the world of Fiona Frost at Fionafrost.com. Fiona Frost is a seventeen-year-old criminal investigator. The Fiona Frost Franchise includes murder mystery party games, murder mystery novels, merchandise, and more. Visit the site for fun forensic challenges and learn more about crime investigation and forensic science. Join Fiona's fan club for fun games and giveaways. Dr. Bon plans to release fifteen volumes of the murder mystery novel series with the second volume being released the summer of 2012.

The following is Dr. Bon's collection:

Connect with Dr. Bon:
Web: bonblossman.com   YouTube: bonblossman
Twitter: BonBlossman   Facebook: Dr. Bon Blossman

For pictures and more antidotes from various chapters, go to bonblossman.com/autobiograph

3761675R00093

Printed in Great Britain
by Amazon.co.uk, Ltd.,
Marston Gate.